The Aviation Notebook !

LOCKHEED

CONSTELLATION

Stewart Wilson

NOTEBOOK PUBLICATIONS
Australia

Foreword

The romance of years gone by was often captured in advertisements and travel posters by the vision of a Lockheed Constellation flying over an exotic location somewhere in the world, places that few would have visited when these majestic airliners entered service. For many, the Constellation represented their dreams of seeing the world, and for some of them, provided the means.

For others - such as aviation enthusiasts and engineering minded people - the Constellation represented a pinnacle of technical achievement which was state-of-the-art when it was introduced. For a large number of people the 'magic' of the Constellation will never go away.

Stewart Wilson's wonderful contribution to the recording of Australian and international aviation history through his beautifully written and well illustrated books has in no small way been an inspiration to many Australians obsessed with the restoration and flight of old aircraft.

As part of the Historical Aircraft Restoration Society I am honoured to write this foreword on behalf of our team which has spent the last 10 years restoring and operating our Lockheed Super Constellation, or 'Connie' as she is affectionately known. She is for all Australians to enjoy and to inspire other groups who take on the enormous task of restoring and flying historic aircraft. Like us, they will have to face the knockers who say 'it can't be done'. Like us, they will prove them wrong and realise there is no such word as 'impossible'.

I'm sure Stewart's new book will add to the enthusiasm for the Constellation, its romance and its technical achievement on the road to safe and reliable commercial air transport as we know it today.

Bob De La Hunty
President and Chief Pilot
Historic Aircraft Restoration Society

The Historic Aircraft Restoration Society's L.1049F/C-121C Super Constellation performs a flypast at the 2001 Australian International Airshow at Avalon. (photo: Dave Crawford)

Contents

Published by Notebook Publications, a division of Wilson Media Pty Ltd (ACN 082 531 066) PO Box 181 Bungendore NSW 2621 Australia; fax +61 2 6238 1626.
Web: www.notebookpub.com

ISBN 1 876722 03 7

Printed in Australia by Pirie Printers Pty Ltd, 140 Gladstone St Fyshwick ACT 2609. Distributed in the United Kingdom and Irish Republic by Airlife Publishing Ltd, 101 Longden Rd Shrewsbury, Shropshire SY3 9EB England. Distributed in North America by MBI Publishing, 729 Prospect Ave, Osceola, Wisconsin 54020 USA.

Production and design: Wendy Wilson
Special thanks to Australian Aviation magazine, Bob De La Hunty and HARS, Eric Allen and David Crawford.
Original colour and line drawings by Juanita Franzi

Front cover: Australia's Historical Aircraft Restoration Society (HARS) restored and operates the former USAF C-121C Super Constellation 54-0157 as VH-EAG 'Southern Preservation'.

Star Of The Skies

In airliner terms it was the battle for the heavyweight championship of the world. For most of the 1950s a fight for market supremacy was waged between the Lockheed and Douglas companies in the long range commercial aircraft division, the battle resulting in development of the 'ultimate' piston engined airliners.

Since the 1930s, Douglas had been the dominant force in the airliner market with the DC-2 and epochal DC-3, followed by the four engined DC-4 and its pressurised derivative for the post war era, the DC-6. From that was developed the long range DC-7 for international services, and it was against this aircraft that the Lockheed Constellation was largely pitted in the post war years..

Initially designed to meet a TWA requirement, the Constellation's early commercial career was interrupted by the global conflict of 1939-45 but when commercial air travel resumed after the war, the 'Connie' was ready to assume a significant role.

From Constellation to Super Constellation and finally Starliner, Lockheed's family of piston engined airliners was developed as far as the *genre* could go - as was the DC-7 - before the jet airliners from Boeing and then Douglas revolutionised commercial air travel at the end of the 1950s.

Total production of the Constellation family reached 856 between the first flight of the prototype in early 1943 and the end of the line in 1958. During that period, 508 new aircraft were delivered from the production line to 34 commercial operators in 18 countries (plus two prototypes) and a substantial 346 went to the US military. There were more than 20 major variants produced and including used aircraft sales, over 80 airlines, charter and freight operators in some 30 countries at some stage flew Constellations or Starliners.

The top 15 commercial operators with the biggest Constellation fleets (taking into account both new and used acquisitions) were TWA with 156 aircraft followed by Eastern Air Lines (79), Air France (62), KLM (46), Pan American (34), BOAC (29, of which only five were purchased brand new), Capitol Airways (22), Qantas (22), Flying Tiger Line (21), Capital Airlines (19), Air India (17), Panair do Brasil (16), Lufthansa (14), Trans-Canada (14) and Trans International (14).

TWA was the airline whose requirements led to the development of the Constellation and was the largest commercial operator with more than 150 in its fleet over the years. This L.1049G Super Constellation is pictured over New York.

This list represents many of the world's major international airlines during the 1950s, but the customer list for the rival DC-7 was equally impressive, including Pan American, South African Airways, Continental, Delta, National, American Airlines, Swissair, Braniff, BOAC, Sabena, Mexicana, Northwest, KLM, Alitalia, SAS and Japan Airlines.

Some operated both the Lockheed and Douglas products but most tended to be loyal to one or the other. Loyalty to Lockheed was tested late in the career of its aircraft when the very long range DC-7C was put into service just under a year ahead of the final Constellation development, the directly competitive Starliner. This gap and the range benefits offered by the DC-7C was sufficient for several traditional Lockheed customers to change, and only three purchased the Starliner.

By then it was largely irrelevant because while Lockheed and Douglas had been fighting amongst themselves for the piston engined market, Boeing had been getting on with the development of the next generation, the 707 jet. When the 707 entered service with Pan American in October 1958 it was all over for the big pistons. Douglas responded with the DC-8 jet but was playing 'catch up', while Lockheed ignored the jet airliner and instead went with the medium range turboprop Electra.

By the end of the 20th century, Lockheed hadn't built an airliner for nearly two decades and Douglas no longer existed.

The Lockheed Commercials

By the mid 1930s, the company founded two decades earlier by brothers Allen and Malcolm Loughead was a well established operation based at Burbank, California. Originally formed as the Loughead Aircraft Manufacturing Company in 1916, the firm was liquidated in 1921 but re-established five years later as the Lockheed Aircraft Company of Hollywood. Its best known product over the next few years was the Vega, a single engined high wing monoplane of wooden construction powered by a Wright Whirlwind or Pratt & Whitney Wasp radial engine of between 225hp (167kW) and 450hp (335kW).

Designed by Jack Northrop, the seven seat Vega was noted for its aerodynamic cleanliness (despite fixed undercarriage) and cantilever wing which removed the need for bracing struts. The first Vega flew in July 1927 and the type was used for many record breaking flights in the late 1920s and early 1930s. The best known of these was Wiley Post's *Winnie Mae* which set two around the world records in 1931 and 1933, the latter the first solo achievement.

The Air Express and low wing Orion continued the line of small, single engined Lockheed transports into the 1930s. The company had established a reputation as a manufacturer offering innovative, high performance designs to the market. The name became linked to record breaking

The US military accounted for 40 per cent of Constellation production. The sole VC-121E (53-7885 *Columbine III*, c/n 4151) was President Eisenhower's 'Air Force 1'.

flights by not only Wiley Post but also the likes of Howard Hughes and Amelia Earhart.

The company's road to more permanent commercial success began with the first of a series of high performance, all metal twin engined aircraft which were developed to meet the needs of commercial air travel in the 1930s.

The L.10 Electra was the first of the new breed, first flying in February 1934 and capable of carrying ten passengers at a speed of close to 200mph (320km/h). Featuring retractable undercarriage, the L.10 was powered by Pratt & Whitney or Wright radial engines of around 450hp (335kW). The Electra was considered advanced for its day and 148 were built, almost all of them for the airlines. Like subsequent Lockheed twins, a distinctive feature of the Electra was its twin endplate fin and rudder assemblies.

Next came the similar in configuration but smaller and faster L.12 Electra Junior, designed to carry six passengers. This first flew in June in 1936 (130 built) and was followed in July 1937 by the much larger L.14 Super Electra. Powered by Pratt & Whitney or Wright radials of 750-900hp (559-671kW), the L.14 was capable of carrying 12-14 passengers. From it came the military Hudson, ordered by the Royal Air Force in large numbers as a maritime patrol/reconnaissance bomber and the aircraft which transformed Lockheed into a major manufacturer.

The first Hudson flew in December 1938, one month before the prototype of the company's first serious attempt at a combat aircraft, the P-38 Lightning twin engined fighter. Both went on to be produced in large numbers.

The last of Lockheed's twin engined commercial line was the 14 passenger L.18 Lodestar (first flight September 1939), an enlarged development of the L.14 and also further developed into patrol bomber versions through the more powerful PV-1 Ventura and PV-2 Harpoon.

In 1937 the Vega Aircraft Corporation was formed as a Lockheed affiliate and in 1941 the company became a wholly owned subsidiary of what was now called simply the Lockheed Aircraft Corporation. The Vega name officially disappeared two years after that, although it remained in general use.

Towards Constellation

1938 was a big year for Lockheed with the British placing an order for 200 L.14 Super Electra military derivatives as the Hudson and the company working on the final design and construction of the prototype XP-38 fighter. It was also the year the company began work on the concepts which would lead to the Constellation airliner.

Early in the year, design studies were instigated for a new four engined

Lockheed moved into the twin engined, all metal field in 1934 with the advanced L.10 Electra. Most of the 148 built went to commercial operators.

(Opposite) The Constellation as it was first conceived in 1939 with completely faired nose and streamlined, reverse flow engine cowlings. Otherwise, the basic configuration was already established.

Drawing of the Model 44 Excalibur project as revealed in April 1939. Designed to carry around 30 passengers, it resembled a scaled up, four engined L.10.

airliner, several concepts emerging with seating capacities ranging up to 42 passengers. In April 1939 the company revealed details of its Model 44 Excalibur powered by four Wright Cyclone or Pratt & Whitney radial engines and featuring the twin tail design which had been applied to the L.10 and L.12. In many ways the new aircraft looked like a scaled up, four engined version of those.

As it was originally presented, the Excalibur was intended to seat 21 passengers, but discussions with the airlines (notably Pan American) resulted in further enlargement and a passenger capacity of 30-36. The project had got to the stage of wind tunnel testing and the building of a

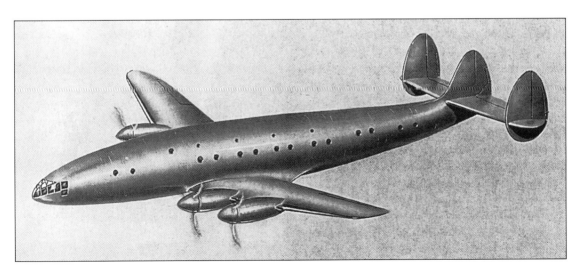

mockup when Transcontinental & Western Air (TWA - Trans World Airlines from 1950) entered the pictured in June 1939.

TWA issued a requirement for an airliner capable of flying transcontinental US services non stop west to east or with one stop travelling in the opposite direction against the prevailing wind. It was required to fly above the weather carrying a 6,000lb (2,720kg) payload while cruising at up to 300mph (483km/h) and had to cover the 2,540 statute miles (4,087km) between Los Angeles and New York in 8-9 hours. Maximum range was to be 3,500 miles (5,632km).

The specification was drawn up by TWA's majority shareholder, multi-millionaire businessman and pilot Howard Hughes and TWA president Jack Frye. It was Hughes who insisted on two major components of the specification - cabin pressurisation and use of the then new Wright R-3350 'Duplex Cyclone' 18-cylinder two row radial engine which promised to produce more than 2,000hp (1,490kW).

The R-3350 was subsequently selected for use in the Boeing B-29 Superfortress bomber and although proving to be a troublesome powerplant in its early days in both that aircraft and the Constellation, it was also an astute choice by Hughes for commercial reasons. Compared with Wright's next biggest engine - the R-2600 Cyclone - the R-3350 produced over 20 per cent more power but also returned 26 per cent lower specific fuel consumption.

The result was the seemingly perfect combination of enhanced performance in combination with lower operating costs, but for a while the R-3350 was the Constellation's Achilles Heel.

Design of the what was called the Lockheed Model 49 (later 049) was undertaken by Lockheed's design team led by vice president and chief engineer Hal Hibbard and the legendary Clarence 'Kelly' Johnson. Don Palmer was the project engineer.

The design they came up with was advanced for its time and highly distinctive with its triple fins and curvy, dolphin shaped circular section fuselage. This aerofoil-like shape was sometimes described as a 'lifting fuselage' and although it did feature a small reduction in drag compared to conventional cylindrical pressurised fuselages, it was also criticised by some for preventing full utilisation of interior space. Lockheed's reasoning behind the shape was that it increased the maximum width of level floor, especially in the nose and tail areas.

The triple fins were not an attempt to continue any family resemblance

Lockheed's twin engined theme developed through the 1930s via the L.12 Electra Junior, the larger L.14 Super Electra and finally the fourteen passenger L.18 Lodestar (illustrated) which first flew in September 1939.

The Constellation's Wright R-3350 engines were tested on this Lockheed PV-1 Ventura patrol bomber, replacing the standard Pratt & Whitney R-2800s. The aircraft was humourously nicknamed Ventillation.

The prototype Lockheed Model 049/C-69 Constellation (c/n 1961) first flew on 9 January 1943 from the company's Burbank, California facility. The aircraft wore military markings but initially carried the civil registration NX25600.

to previous Lockheed airliners, but merely a practical solution to one of TWA's requirements - that the new airliner should be able to fit into existing maintenance hangars. A conventional single vertical tail would have been too tall to achieve this.

By 1939 the general configuration and shape of the Model 49 was established except that the conventional stepped windscreen design which appeared on the finished article was nowhere to be seen. Instead, the nose was completely faired with cockpit glazing at its extremity and no step. Two separate 'bug eye' canopies for the pilot and copilot were also investigated but dropped. Another feature which would disappear was the use of streamlined engine cowlings and large, flush fitting propeller spinners with the engines cooled by a reverse airflow system.

Despite, these omissions, the Model 49 still bristled with innovation and advanced features: it was the first airliner with reversible-pitch propellers (a major safety breakthrough for landing on contaminated runways), the first transport with hydraulically boosted flight controls, the cabin was pressurised and tricycle undercarriage was fitted.

The stalky, rearwards retracting and 9ft 6in (2.9m) long nosewheel leg was a feature of all Constellations and resulted from the need to provide sufficient ground clearance for the large, 15ft 2in (4.62m) diameter three bladed propellers. Even so, the leg was shorter than it could have been as when the stepped windscreen design was adopted, the nose area was drooped slightly to keep it a minimum.

The Constellation's wing was interesting in that it was a direct scaling up of the design used on the P-38 fighter. Low speed control was helped by the fitting of the large area increasing Fowler flaps which were also a feature of the L.14 Super Electra , L.18 Lodestar and P-38. Overall construction of the Model 49 was metal with fabric covered control surfaces.

A rudder was fitted to each of the three vertical fins.

Flight crew accommodation was four-five with two pilots, radio operator and flight engineer in the main cockpit and space for a navigator behind the cockpit bulkhead. A crew rest area was also provided opposite the navigator's position. The engineer was an integral part of the flight crew, his job going far beyond merely monitoring the aircraft's systems.

The engineer's position included controls for the engine throttles, superchargers, fuel mixture and other functions. These were operated by the engineer throughout all phases of the flight from startup to final approach when the pilots took over the throttles themselves. At other times the engineer manipulated these at the pilots' call, reducing their workload as well as being able to keep a close eye on the sometimes cantankerous engines' state of health.

Passenger accommodation was initially set at 60 first class passengers or up to 22 berths and four seats on the full sleeper version. Very few were equipped with this extent of sleeper accommodation. Passengers viewed the world through circular cabin windows in the early versions, this changing to a greater number of larger rectangular windows in the stretched Super Constellation.

A more detailed description of the Constellation's technical features appears later in the chapter.

The prototype during an early flight. It was grounded in February 1943 following the crash of a Boeing B-29 due to an uncontained fire in one of its R-3350 engines, the same powerplant used in the Constellation.

First Orders

TWA placed its first order for nine Model 049s in early 1940 with another 40 added later, followed by Pan American (40) and the Netherlands' KLM (4) shortly afterwards. The TWA and KLM orders were for the basic L.049 model while Pan American's was subsequently revised to cover both the L.049 and the proposed longer range L.349. By now, the war against Germany in Europe and elsewhere had started in earnest and although the USA wasn't as yet involved, the feeling was that it soon would be. As a result, there was considerable doubt that these orders would be fulfilled. Events were to prove this to be the case, at least for a time.

Lockheed began construction of the prototype L.049 immediately after the TWA order had been placed but had already began looking at possible military developments in view of the world situation.

Even before the Japanese attack on Pearl Harbour on 7 December 1941 and the USA's formal involvement in World War II, the country's industries were pretty much on a war footing with production of aircraft and other armaments increasing rapidly for Britain, its allies and the US itself. Airliners were being impressed into US military service directly off the production line and the business of commercial air transport became heavily controlled.

It became clear that the Lockheed Constellation would not be able to go directly into worldwide commercial service as planned. With the Netherlands invaded by Germany, KLM's order obviously lapsed and when Japan attacked Pearl Harbour both TWA and Pan American waived all their rights associated with the Constellation in favour of the USAAF. On 9 September 1942 the USAAF signed a contract for the purchase of 260 Constellations as the C-69.

Flying Into Problems

The prototype had been completed by November 1942, it was weighed on the 16th of that month, engine runs took place two days later and initial taxying runs were conducted on the 20th. Six weeks in the workshop for systems checks were followed by a planned first flight on 5 January 1943.

This event had to be delayed by four days due to a combination of bad weather and the late arrival of experienced and highly regarded test pilot Eddie Allen, who was on loan from Boeing. Wearing military camouflage and markings but carrying the civil registration NX25600, the first Constellation (c/n 1961) took to the air on 9 January 1943 from Burbank.

Early flights resulted in modifications to the flight control power boost system, hydraulic hoses (following a broken hydraulic line), while stronger

Cockpit of a Super Constellation, in this case a C-121C. The flight engineer's station is behind the co-pilot's seat on the right hand side, while the radio operator was located behind the captain.

wing spar caps and stainless steel flame shields were fitted to the engine nacelles and undercarriage doors.

Eleven flights had been completed by 20 February 1943, at which point the prototype was grounded following the crash two days earlier of the second B-29 Superfortress. The crash killed Eddie Allen, his crew and 19 people on the ground and was caused by an uncontained fire in one of the B-29's R-3350 engines.

Fires and other failures continued to dog the R-3350 well into 1944 before a solution was found, the major problems eventually discovered to be excessive cylinder head temperatures resulting from poorly lubricated valves and a faulty fuel induction system design which resulted in the fires. The first B-29 suffered a fire in 1944, but quick extinguishing of it meant the engine could be examined after landing. Previously, the evidence had been destroyed by the fire itself.

These problems were developing even before the prototype Constellation flew and studies into substituting the reliable Pratt & Whitney R-2800 Double Wasp for the Wright R-3350 had been conducted at an early stage. The R-2800 never made it onto production Constellations but the prototype was later fitted with the engine and redesignated XC-69E, as described in the next chapter.

While it was grounded in early 1943 the prototype had more modifications incorporated including a strengthened nosewheel leg, reinforced wing root fillets and outer leading edges, the cabin pressurisation and heating systems were fitted and de-icing boots and a Sperry autopilot installed. Modified engines were also installed and it wasn't until mid June 1943 that the aircraft flew again.

It was delivered to the USAAF for service trials in July with the military serial number 43-10309. By that stage the C-69 Constellation programme for the USAAF was already being subject to cutbacks, delays and a loss of priority. The second Constellation (C-69 43-10310, c/n 1962) first flew in August 1943.

Despite the technical and political issues that were inhibiting the C-69 programme in 1943-44, the aircraft quickly proved that its performance capabilities were outstanding. Testing of the first two aircraft revealed a maximum speed of 347mph (558km/h), this faster than any contemporary four engined bomber including - marginally - the B-29 and better than some fighters. The intended high speed cruise of 275mph (442km/h) was achieved using only 52.5 per cent power, this in turn helping the aircraft meet its design fuel consumption goal of one statute mile per US gallon. Payload-range performance was also better than predicted.

Technical Aspects

The following is a brief description of the Constellation's main technical characteristics. It applies generally to all models except where specifically noted.

Wings: Cantilever all metal structure in five (L.049-749) or seven (L.1049) main sections comprising a centre section, two outer sections and detachable tips (L.049-749) or a centre section, two inner and two outer sections with detachable tips (L.1049). Two spar structure with flush rivetted stressed metal skins; false spar carrying ailerons and flaps; metal ailerons with fabric (L.049-749) or metal (L.1049) covering with trim tab and hydraulic boost; Fowler trailing edge area increasing flaps.

Fuselage: All metal semi-monocoque; circular cross section with centreline cambered for aerodynamic 'aerofoil' shape; structure featured transverse frames and flush rivetted stressed metal skinning.

Tail Unit: All metal cantilever tailplane with stressed metal skinning on fixed surfaces and two piece fabric covered elevator. Three vertical fins of similar construction with fabric covered rudders; elevators and rudders hydraulically boosted and fitted with trim tabs.

Undercarriage: Retractable tricycle type with dual wheels on all units; steerable nosewheel; dual hydraulic brake system with auxiliary manual override on mainwheels.

Powerplants: Four Wright R-3350 Cyclone or Turbo Compound 18-cylinder two row air cooled radial piston engines of between 2,200hp (1,640kW) and 3,400hp (2,535kW); see individual models for details. Fully feathering and reversible Hamilton Standard Hydromatic or Curtiss Electric three bladed propellers of 15ft 2in (4.62m) diameter. Fuel in wing, centre section and tip tanks with capacities between 4,760 USgal (18,018 l) and 7,750 USgal (29,337 l) in L.049-L.1049; see individual models for details. Total oil capacity 186 USgal (704 l) in four tanks (L.049-749) or 227 USgal (859 l) in five tanks (L.1049).

Accommodation: Pressurised, heated and air conditioned cockpit and cabin; pressurisation system allows 8,000ft cabin altitude when aircraft flying at 20,000ft (L.049-749) or 8,000ft cabin at 22,800ft (L.1049). Normal flight crew four-five, passenger capacity 44-95 (see individual models); underfloor luggage capacity 440cu ft (12.5m^3) on L.049-749 or 728cu ft (20.6m^3) on L.1049. Optional underfuselage 'Speedpak' freight pannier on L.049-749 models of 395cu ft (11.2m^3) capacity.

Early L.749 Constellations on the production line at Burbank.

C-69 and L.049 Constellation

On 9 September 1942 the USAAF signed a contract for the purchase of 260 C-69 Constellations. These comprised 50 basic C-69s from the TWA and Pan American orders which had been taken over by the military when the USA entered the war in December 1941, 30 C-69As (also from former civil orders) and 180 newly ordered C-69Bs.

In the event, the vast majority were cancelled and only 21 were built for the USAAF comprising 20 C-69s and one C-69C. Even then, only the C-69C and 13 C-69s entered limited USAAF service, the remainder cancelled before delivery and going instead to the British Overseas Airways Corporation (5) and TWA (2) in late 1945-early 1946.

The second Constellation off the line was also the first production C-69 (43-10310, c/n 1962). It first flew in August 1943 at a time when the programme was already starting to suffer from the reliability problems which were plaguing the R-3350 engine.

The planned C-69 variants were:

C-69: Based on the Model 049 airliner airframe and powered by four 2,200hp (1,640kW) Wright R-3350-18 radial engines. The interior was finished to a relatively austere military standard with 44 individual seats and four folding benches each capable of seating four. Initial maximum takeoff weight was 65,000lb (29,484kg), subsequently increasing to 72,000lb (32,659kg).

The first C-69 (43-10310) flew in August 1943 and was delivered to the USAAF in April 1944 after flying in both TWA and Pan Am colours while carrying its military serial number. After the various order cancellations which occurred in 1944-45, only 13 aircraft were completed to basic C-69 standards for the USAAF, the final example in September 1945.

C-69A: Proposed version with high density seating for 100 troops and equipped with a large cargo door. Orders cancelled and none built.

Pan Am inaugurated Constellation commercial services on 3 February 1946 with a New York-Bermuda flight using an L.049. This L.049 is N88832 *Clipper Flora Temple* (c/n 2032), delivered to Pan Am in February 1946 and later converted to an L.149.

C-69B: Proposed longer range version of C-69A with additional fuel capacity and maximum takeoff weight increased to 86,000lb (39,010kg). Orders cancelled and none built.

C-69C: One aircraft (42-94550, c/n 1971) completed as a VIP transport with additional cabin windows and accommodation for 42 passengers. The C-69C was delivered to the USAAF in August 1945, leased to TWA for a month in June 1946 and then sold to BOAC in August 1947. The aircraft was converted to L.049D and then L.049E standards while in BOAC service before being sold to Capital Airlines in June 1955.

C-69D: Proposed version with 57 seats and increased maximum weight. Not built.

The C-69 programme was always running well behind schedule and apart from the engine and other mechanical problems there were administrative delays resulting from the need to renegotiate contracts to cover the extra costs incurred in fixing those problems.

In addition, by mid 1943 the USAAF was beginning to receive large numbers of the four engined Douglas C-54, a military version of the commercial DC-4. Although unpressurised, the C-54 offered reasonable speed, range and payload, was relatively inexpensive, reliable and most importantly, available in quantity when most needed. Deliveries began in June 1942 and the C-54 was soon flying regular services on USAAF transport routes around the world including across the Atlantic to Britain, the Pacific to Australia plus Africa, China, India and elsewhere.

Like the Constellation, the DC-4 had been conceived and developed for the civil market before the USA was involved in the war. It first flew in February 1942 and was also taken over by the USAAF, which received nearly 1,000.

The ready availability of the C-54 contributed to the USAAF taking a hard look at the C-69 programme and making cuts. In June 1943 it was decided that production would be at a reduced rate, covering 98 aircraft before the end of 1944. Overall, the contracts still covered the eventual purchase of 260 aircraft but the C-69B was dropped.

The delivery schedule was further downgraded to cover 79 aircraft by the end of 1944. With problems continuing, costs increasing, entry to service date slipping and the immediate need for the C-69 diminishing, the contracts were regularly cut.

Total planned procurement was reduced to 210 in June 1943, 79 in April 1945 and finally only 21 in October 1945 after the cessation of hostilities. As noted above, only 14 were ultimately delivered to the USAAF,

The first production C-69 (43-10310, c/n 1962), first flown in August 1943 and delivered to the USAAF eight months later. It shared in much of the early constellation development work and also flew in both Pan Am and TWA colours at some stage.

the other seven went to commercial operators and airframes originally intended for the military were completed as commercial L.049s for post war delivery.

Overall C-69/L.049 production reached 88 aircraft.

Limited Service

The first C-69 delivered to the USAAF was handed over in April 1944 and as a result of the cutbacks and uncertainties surrounding the programme, further deliveries were at a leisurely pace and ended in September 1945 after a low priority effort. By the end of 1944 only three had been handed over with others built but delayed because of the need to rectify the long list of problems.

No fewer than 486 different modifications were required to make the aircraft acceptable for USAAF service. In order to perform the 'fixes', Lockheed established an outdoor modification line at its Burbank Customer Service Centre.

The situation got so bad that in June 1944 the USAAF issued a directive banning the small number of aircraft then flying from travelling outside the USA.

This ban was eventually lifted and the newly delivered C-69 42-94551 (c/n 1972) made some history on 4 August 1945 when it recorded the first trans-Atlantic flight by a Constellation, travelling from New York to Paris non stop in the record time of 14hrs 12 min.

Unfortunately, the same aircraft made a different kind of history the following month when it became the first Constellation involved in a major accident. Another uncontained fire in one of the C-69's R-3350 engines was the cause, and although the aircraft was successfully force landed in a field near Topeka, Kansas, it was destroyed by fire on the ground. The crew escaped safely.

This incident resulted in another grounding and another raft of mandatory modifications before the Constellation was allowed back into service.

The C-69 Constellation's career with USAAF Air Transport Command was a generally unhappy and short one which saw the aircraft never used on a regular basis and in the intended long range transport role.

The survivors were declared surplus to requirements shortly after the war ended and sold to civil operators in 1947-48, these including Lineas Aereas de Panama, Intercontinent Airways, Capital Airlines and TWA. One aircraft (43-10314, c/n 1966) was damaged beyond repair in an accident before it could be sold, while 42-94552 (c/n 1973) was static tested to destruction at Wright Field, Ohio in 1946. The sole C-69C went to TWA and then BOAC.

43-10317 was the eighth C-69 (c/n 1969), delivered in April 1945 when the whole military Constellation programme was enduring technical problems and contract cuts. This aircraft went to TWA after the war.

The outdoor Constellation modification line at the Lockheed Air Terminal Customer Service Centre at Burbank. Nearly 500 modifications were required to make the aircraft acceptable for USAAF service.

The XC-69E

One early Constellation which survived to go onto a long and useful life was the original prototype. As a C-69 (43-10309) it had been delivered to the USAAF in July 1943 and been used for various tests and trials as well as the general Constellation development programme.

In early 1945 'Old 1961' (as it became known, after its constructor's number) had its Wright R-3350 engines replaced with 2,400hp (1,790kW) Pratt & Whitney R-2800 Double Wasps following a USAAF request for a comparative evaluation between the two powerplants. The new designation XC-69E was applied and the tests revealed no long term advantages in powering future Constellations with the R-2800.

The XC-69E was withdrawn from service in March 1946 and stored at Burbank before being sold to Howard Hughes as NC25600 the following August, in whose hands it logged fewer than 100 hours flying time over the next 45 months.

Hughes had purchased the number one Connie for only $US20,000 but he sold the aircraft to Lockheed in May 1950 for $US100,000. By then, it had the grand total of 404 hours in its logbook.

Lockheed's reacquisition of 'Old 1961' heralded a new career for the aircraft, the manufacturer rebuilding it as the prototype stretched L.1049 Super Constellation. In that form it recorded its second 'first flight' on 13 October 1950, still powered by the Pratt & Whitney engines.

Civil L.049s

The end of World War II and the cancellation of military contracts left most major US aircraft manufacturers with the need to develop programmes which would tide them over in the post war world. Lockheed was no exception and had the added problem of a stock of seven already built but undelivered C-69s originally intended for the USAAF and many others on the production line.

The decision was therefore taken to relaunch the Constellation on the civil market under its original L.049 designation. There was considerable financial risk in this venture for the company as it involved not only committing the aircraft to further production but also repurchasing the seven undelivered C-69s plus some others which had already been delivered but were surplus to USAAF requirements.

They would be refurbished as civil L.049s and resold in the months after the war had ended. This not only provided work for Lockheed's employees but also got the commercial Constellation into service nearly a year ahead of the rival Douglas DC-6, and with a healthy list of orders.

L.049: The commercial version of the military C-69 was awarded its Type Certificate on 14 October 1945 following the introduction of a series of modifications required under civil rules. These included installation of an engine fire detection and extinguisher system, a very necessary inclusion given the R-3350 powerplant's previous history.

Other modifications reflected the Constellation's commercial role and included appropriate interior furnishings and configurations plus some additional cabin windows. Maximum takeoff weight of the L.049 was

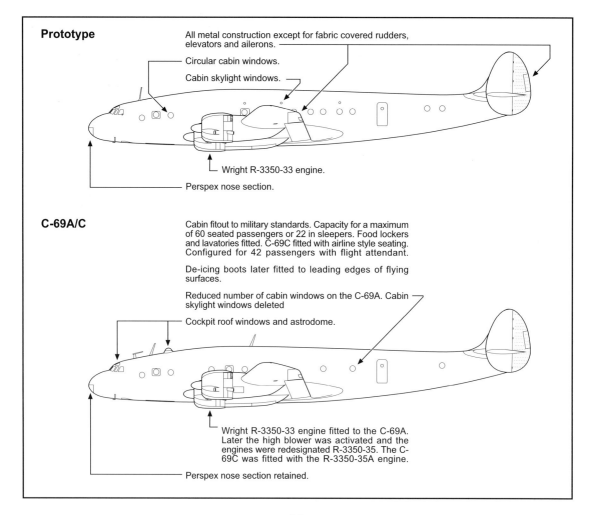

Prototype

All metal construction except for fabric covered rudders, elevators and ailerons.

Circular cabin windows.

Cabin skylight windows.

Wright R-3350-33 engine.

Perspex nose section.

C-69A/C

Cabin fitout to military standards. Capacity for a maximum of 60 seated passengers or 22 in sleepers. Food lockers and lavatories fitted. C-69C fitted with airline style seating. Configured for 42 passengers with flight attendant.

De-icing boots later fitted to leading edges of flying surfaces.

Reduced number of cabin windows on the C-69A. Cabin skylight windows deleted

Cockpit roof windows and astrodome.

Wright R-3350-33 engine fitted to the C-69A. Later the high blower was activated and the engines were redesignated R-3350-35. The C-69C was fitted with the R-3350-35A engine.

Perspex nose section retained.

86,250lb (39,123kg), more than 14,000lb (6,350kg) heavier than the C-69. A modification introduced well into the L.049's production run was replacing the original free castoring nosewheel with a properly steerable unit.

Three different powerplant options were available to prospective purchasers: the standard 2,200hp (1,640kW) Wright R-3350-C18-BA1 Cyclone; the 2,400hp (1,790kW) Pratt & Whitney R-2800 Double Wasp (as installed on the XC-69E conversion of the prototype); and the 2,300hp (1,715kW) Bristol Centaurus. All customers opted for the R-3350.

By late 1945 Lockheed had booked orders for 103 L.049 Constellations from eight operators. Not all were filled as some opted to wait for the dedicated commercial L.649/749 models which would appear from 1947. L.049 deliveries reached 73 aircraft, for Air France (4), American Overseas Airlines (7), BOAC (5), KLM (6), Linea Aeropostal Venezolana (2), Pan American (20), Pan American Grace (Panagra, 2) and TWA (27). The final delivery was to TWA in May 1947.

Pan American was responsible for inaugurating Constellation commercial flights on 3 February 1946 when a New York-Bermuda service was flown. This was followed by a New York-London service eight days later, the precursor of regular trans-Atlantic operations.

TWA quickly followed, inaugurating a New York-Paris service on 6 February 1946, although the airline had operated a proving flight between the two cities the previous December, stopping at Gander and Shannon on the way.

Coast-to coast US domestic operations were equally important for American airlines, TWA starting the ball rolling with the introduction of a New York-Los Angeles service on 15 February 1946. Some non stop west-east flights were performed but with reduced payload; in normal operations one stop was required in both directions.

On 17 June 1947 Pan American L.049 N88858 *Clipper America* (c/n 2058) departed New York at the start of the world's first around-the-world air service. Over the next 14 days the Constellation travelled to Gander, Shannon, London, Istanbul, Dhahran, Karachi, Calcutta, Bangkok, Manila, Shanghai, Tokyo, Guam, Wake Island, Midway, Honolulu and San Francisco before returning to New York.

Eleven years later, Australia's Qantas launched the first *scheduled* around-the-world services using L.1049G Super Constellations.

The L.049's introduction to commercial service was not without its dramas.

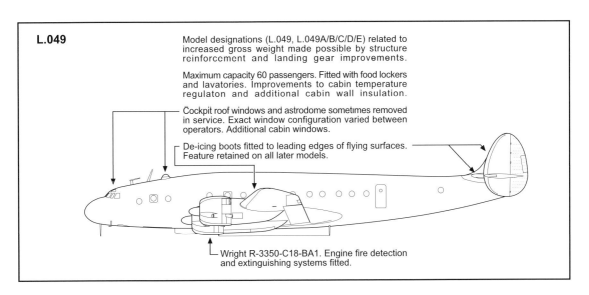

L.049

Model designations (L.049, L.049A/B/C/D/E) related to increased gross weight made possible by structure reinforcement and landing gear improvements.

Maximum capacity 60 passengers. Fitted with food lockers and lavatories. Improvements to cabin temperature regulaton and additional cabin wall insulation.

Cockpit roof windows and astrodome sometimes removed in service. Exact window configuration varied between operators. Additional cabin windows.

De-icing boots fitted to leading edges of flying surfaces. Feature retained on all later models.

Wright R-3350-C18-BA1. Engine fire detection and extinguishing systems fitted.

The fleet was grounded in mid July 1946 after two incidents involving in-flight fires in Pan Am and TWA aircraft. Neither was directly related to the engines (one involved ancillaries and the other electrics) but the groundings kept the aircraft out of service for a month while modifications were incorporated.

Increased operating weights were permitted for the L.049 from 1950 with the introduction of some structural and undercarriage strengthening, these modifications available for retrofit.

New designation suffixes were introduced to denote increased maximum takeoff weights: L.049A - 90,000lb (40,824kg); L.049B/C - 93,000lb (42,185kg); L.049D - 96,000lb (43,545kg); L.049E: 98,000lb (44,453kg). No aircraft were upgraded to L.049A, B or C standards but 13 were converted to L.049Ds and six to L.049Es.

L.149: A model designation applied twice, the first in 1940 for a proposed but unbuilt lightweight version of the L.049 powered by four 875hp (652kW) Wright R-1820 Cyclone engines. The second use of the L.149 designation was post war when Lockheed offered a modification of the

TWA L.049 N90831 ***Star of Switzerland,*** **the former USAAF 42-94549 (c/n 1970) and the 10th Constellation off the line. Delivered to the USAAF in April 1945, it went to TWA in October 1948.**

Eleven L.049 Constellations were converted to L.149 standards with additional fuel tanks in the outer wings. El Al's 4X-AKA was one of them, this aircraft starting life in late 1944 as the fourth production C-69 (43-10313, c/n 1965). It was purchased by The Jewish Agency for El Al in late 1949.

L.049 with additional fuel tankage in the outer wings. Eleven aircraft were modified to L.149 standards.

L.249: A July 1940 design study for a long heavy bomber version of the L.049 to contest the requirement which resulted in the USAAF ordering the Boeing B-29. Equipped with five gun turrets and a bomb bay within the fuselage, the design was allocated the USAAF designation XB-30 but did not progress beyond the drawing board.

L.349: Designation applied to a long range version of the L.049 ordered by Pan American in 1940. It was taken over by the USAAF as the C-69B but not built.

L.449/549: Design studies for post war commercial versions of the L.049/C-69, both superceded by the L.649.

(Opposite) American Overseas Airlines received NC90922 *Flagship Copenhagen* (c/n 2052) - the first of its seven L.049s - in March 1946. AOA flew from the USA to Scandinavia, Germany and Iceland and was later taken over by Pan Am.

L.049 CONSTELLATION

Powerplants: Four 2,200hp (1,640kW) Wright R-3350-C18-BA1 Cyclone 18-cylinder radials; Hamilton-Standard or Curtiss Electric three bladed propellers of 15ft 2in (4.62m) diameter. Fuel capacity 4,760 USgal (18,018 l) in four wing tanks.

Dimensions: Wing span 123ft 0in (37.49m); length 95ft 3in (29.03m); height 23ft 8in (7.21m); wing area 1650sq ft (153.3m²).

Weights: Empty 49,400lb (22,408kg); max takeoff 86,250lb (39,123kg); max landing 75,000lb (34,020kg); max payload 18,420lb (8,355kg).

Accommodation: Typically 43-48 passengers, maximum 60. Cabin length 64ft 9in (19.73m), height 6ft 6in (1.98m), width 10ft 8.6in (3.26m). Underfloor freight/luggage capacity 440cu ft (12.46m³).

Performance: Max speed 294kt (545km/h); max cruise 272kt (504km/h); normal cruise 239kt (442km/h); service ceiling 25,300ft; range 1,990nm (3,686km) with 18,400lb (8,346kg) payload, 3,200nm (5,925km) with 7,800lb (3,538kg) payload.

L.649/749 Constellation

With the war over, the L.049 Constellation's airline career finally got properly underway in February 1946 when Pan American inaugurated services on the New York-Bermuda route. Lockheed was now able to turn its attention to the development of true commercial versions of the aircraft.

With a boom in air travel predicted for the post war years, Lockheed looked to developing new Constellation models which would be suitable for both international and medium range US domestic services. It was the start of the last 'golden age' for piston engined airliners with Lockheed and Douglas entering into fierce competition for market supremacy over the next decade until the jets began to enter service.

The quest for more speed, more range and more passenger capacity was an ongoing battle, Lockheed offering continual development of the Constellation through the Super Constellation and finally Starliner families, these pitted against strong opposition from the Douglas DC-6 and DC-7 models.

The race pushed radial piston engine development to its limit and in some cases beyond, resulting in extraordinary power outputs but at the same time reliability problems.

Lockheed's first post war Constellations shared the same dimensions as the L.049/C-69 models and were built in several versions:

L.649: Developed to meet an Eastern Air Lines requirement for a medium range airliner, the L.649 Constellation differed from the L.049 in having more powerful 2,500hp (1,864kW) R-3350-C18-BD engines, revised engine cowlings and propellers and an increased maximum takeoff weight of 94,000lb (42,638kg). Fuel capacity remained as before.

The cabin environment underwent considerable enhancement in an effort to improve noise and vibration levels and to provide standards of comfort considered to be more in keeping with peacetime commercial requirements. Modified ventilation, heating and air conditioning systems were installed along with wall panels comprising several layers of fibreglass insulation, fire resistant fabrics and air spaces.

With the war over, Lockheed was able to develop true commercial versions of the Constellation, starting with the L.649 and L.749. PH-TFD (c/n 2640) was one of nine L.749As delivered to KLM from October 1948, these preceded by 11 L.749s.

An interesting idea was separating the interior and exterior skins by the use of rubber mountings. The result was a further reduction in noise and vibration. Passenger accommodation was normally 48-64, although later high density arrangements allowed a maximum of 81.

The L.649 represented a substantial redesign over the L.049/C-69 but was purchased only by Eastern. TWA, KLM and Air France all placed orders but these were subsequently changed to the longer range L.749.

The first L.649 (N101A, c/n 2518) flew on 19 October 1946 and was retained by Lockheed before delivery to Eastern in October 1947. The other 13 aircraft were handed over to the airline between March and August 1947. One was damaged beyond repair when it suffered an undercarriage collapse at Boston in January 1948 but all the others were converted to L.749A standards in 1950. Eastern disposed of its 12 surviving L.649/749As in January 1961.

L.649A: Some of the structural strengthening modifications developed for the longer range L.749 (see below) were applied to the L.649, resulting in the L.649A with an increased maximum takeoff weight of 98,000lb (44,453kg) and enhanced payload-range performance.

Only six were built for Chicago & Southern Airlines, the first of them (N86521, c/n 2642) delivered in August 1950. The others followed between then and May 1951. All were converted to L.749A standards after Chicago & Southern was taken over by Delta Air Lines in May 1953. The aircraft were sold in 1954-55 to TWA (3) and Pacific Northern Airlines (3).

L.749: The L.749 Constellation was developed simultaneously with the medium range L.649 and largely in response to the Douglas DC-6 which had first flown in February 1946. In some areas of its performance - notably range - the DC-6 was superior to the L.049/649 models.

The basic changes incorporated in the L.749 were structural and undercarriage modifications which allowed a further increase in maximum takeoff weight to 102,000lb (46,267kg), and an additional 1,555 USgal (5,886 l) of fuel in the outer wings, bringing total capacity to 6,315 USgal (23,904 l).

The result was 780nm (1,445km) more range than the L.649 while carrying the same payload, this sufficient to allow non stop flights between New York and Paris, a distance of 3,180nm (5,890km).

Basic accommodation remained as per the L.649 but sleeping berths were available for long range overnight operations as was the provision to carry a relief crew on these flights at the expense of some passenger capacity.

L.749 production was 51, initially delivered to Air France (9), Aerlinte Eireann (5), Air India (3), KLM (11), LAV (2), Pan Am (4), Qantas (4) and TWA (12), plus the first aircraft (N6520, c/n 2503) which was leased by Lockheed to Pan American and Guest Aerovias Mexico in 1947-48 before being sold to Air France in January 1949.

Air France was the first to take delivery of the L.749 in March 1947 (F-BAZR, c/n 2513), while the last (N91212, c/n 2588) was handed over to TWA in June 1948. Several operators (Qantas, Air France, Eastern, Pan Am, Aerlinte Eireann and KLM) upgraded their L.749 fleets to L.749A standards in 1950-52, a total of 28 aircraft being redesignated.

L.749A: A further increase in maximum takeoff weight to 107,000lb (48,535kg) resulted in the L.749A. Air India received its first of four (VT-CQR, c/n 2505) in February 1948 followed by KLM (9), TWA (25), Air France (10), South African Airways (4), Eastern (7), Avianca (2) and the Hughes Tool Company (1, this later going to BOAC) for a total of 62 commercial models. Twenty-eight L.749s were converted to L.749A standards.

Ten military versions based on the L.749A went to the US Air Force as the C-121A and two PO-1Ws were delivered to the US Navy as airborne early warning (AEW) aircraft with radar mounted in a large radome above the fuselage. These L.749-based military variants are discussed in the next chapter.

The last L.749A (F-BBDV, c/n 2677) was delivered to Air France in September 1951 as the 233rd and last 'short fuselage' Constellation. By then, the first stretched L.1049 Super Constellations were making their way down the production line.

L.849: Proposal for a version of the L.749 powered by the 3,250hp (2,423kW) R-3350-TC18-DA1 Turbo Compound engine as later installed in the L.1049C Super Constellation. Not built.

L.949: 1948-49 design studies into a stretched Constellation with an 11ft 10in (3.60m) longer fuselage, maximum takeoff weight of 123,000lb (55,793kg), 3,250hp (2,423kW) Turbo Compound engines and accommodation for 70 passengers in international configuration. A 'Speedfreighter' all cargo version with 5,000cu ft (141.5m³) of cargo space was also envisaged. The L.949 concept was not developed, Lockheed instead moving on to the

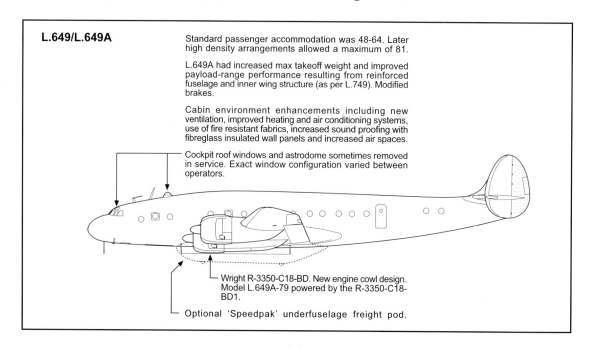

L.649/L.649A

Standard passenger accommodation was 48-64. Later high density arrangements allowed a maximum of 81.

L.649A had increased max takeoff weight and improved payload-range performance resulting from reinforced fuselage and inner wing structure (as per L.749). Modified brakes.

Cabin environment enhancements including new ventilation, improved heating and air conditioning systems, use of fire resistant fabrics, increased sound proofing with fibreglass insulated wall panels and increased air spaces.

Cockpit roof windows and astrodome sometimes removed in service. Exact window configuration varied between operators.

Wright R-3350-C18-BD. New engine cowl design. Model L.649A-79 powered by the R-3350-C18-BD1.

Optional 'Speedpak' underfuselage freight pod.

Capitol Airways L.749A N4901C (c/n 2671) photographed in 1965. This aircraft was the seventh last 749 built and was originally delivered to the Hughes Tool Co in 1951 before going to BOAC in 1954. Note the non standard radar nose.

further stretched L.1049 which achieved production as the Super Constellation.

Speedpak: The 'Speedpak' was an underfuselage freight pod developed at the request of Eastern Air Lines and made available for all standard fuselage Constellations from the last few L.049s onwards. It had a volume of 395cu ft ($11.2m^3$) and could carry a load of up to 8,300lb (3,765kg) within its 33ft (10.0m) length, 7ft (2.1m) width and 3ft (0.9m) depth. Installed weight was 1,800lb (816kg).

Features included a self contained electric hoist which lowered the Speedpak to the ground for loading or unloading and then raised it again when the job was complete. Wheels on the pod's undersides facilitated easy ground handling.

The Speedpak was first tested on the last C-69 delivered to the USAF (42-94558, c/n 1979) and found to have no adverse effects on handling. Speed was reduced by about 10 knots (19km/h) with the pod fitted and range reduced by a proportionate amount. Operationally, this was no problem as use of the Speedpak swapped range for additional payload and it was normally used on short-medium range operations. Several airlines had Speedpaks available for fitting to their Constellations.

L.749/L.749A

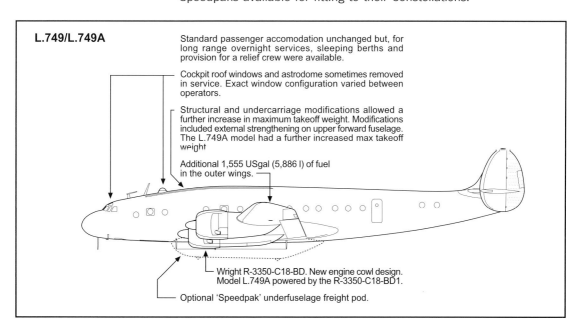

Standard passenger accomodation unchanged but, for long range overnight services, sleeping berths and provision for a relief crew were available.

Cockpit roof windows and astrodome sometimes removed in service. Exact window configuration varied between operators.

Structural and undercarriage modifications allowed a further increase in maximum takeoff weight. Modifications included external strengthening on upper forward fuselage. The L.749A model had a further increased max takeoff weight

Additional 1,555 USgal (5,886 l) of fuel in the outer wings.

Wright R-3350-C18-BD. New engine cowl design. Model L.749A powered by the R-3350-C18-BD1.

Optional 'Speedpak' underfuselage freight pod.

L.649 and L.749/A CONSTELLATION

Powerplants: Four 2,500hp (1,864kW) Wright R-3350-C18-BD Cyclone 18-cylinder radials; Hamilton-Standard or Curtiss Electric three bladed propellers of 15ft 2in (4.62m) diameter. Fuel capacity (L.649) 4,760 USgal (18,018 l) in four wing tanks or (L.749/A) 6,315 USgal (23,905 l) in wing tanks.

Dimensions: Wing span 123ft 0in (37.49m); length 95ft 3in (29.03m) or 97ft 4in (29.67m) with radar nose; height 23ft 8in (7.21m); wing area 1650sq ft (153.3m²).

Weights: L.649 - operational empty 55,000-60,750lb (24,948-27,556kg); max takeoff 94,000lb (42,638kg); max landing 84,500lb (38,329kg); max payload 20,276lb (9,197kg).

L.649A - max takeoff 98,000lb (44,453kg).

L.749 - max takeoff 102,000lb (46,267kg).

L.749A - operational empty 60,140lb (27,280kg); max takeoff 107,000lb (48,535kg); max landing 89,500lb (40,597kg); max payload 20,276lb (9,197kg).

Accommodation: Typically 43-48 passengers on international services or 64 on domestic services; maximum 81 in high density arrangement. Overnight configuration convertible to 20-22 sleeper berths and 4 seats. Cabin length 64ft 9in (19.73m); height 6ft 6in (1.98m); max width 10ft 8.6in (3.26m). Under-floor freight/luggage capacity 440cu ft (12.46m³) and 5,850lb (2,653kg) or 13,400lb (6,078kg) with auxiliary flooring.

Performance: L.649 - max speed 306kt (566km/h); cruising speed 284kt (526km/h); service ceiling 25,700ft; max range 3,740nm (6,430km).

L.749A - max speed 300kt (555km/h); cruising speed 259kt (480km/h); service ceiling 24,100ft; max payload range 2,260nm (4,185km); max fuel range 4,210nm (7,798km).

A 'Speedpak' freight pod being winched up to the lower fuselage of a TWA Constellation. Note the small wheels under the pod for ground manoeuvring. It had a capacity of 395cu ft (11.2m³) and could carry up to 8,300lb (3,765kg) of cargo.

Military L.749 Variants

The development of the post war L.749 Constellation models once again made the aircraft an attractive proposition for the US military, combining enhanced performance and load carrying capability with a degree of reliability which was considerably greater than had been experienced with the original L.049/C-69s.

The United States Army Air Force (USAAF) became the independent US Air Force (USAF) on 18 September 1947 and in February 1948 the service ordered 10 L.749s under the designation C-121, this differentiating the new aircraft from the earlier C-69s despite the new aircraft being direct developments of the originals.

The Constellations were allocated the USAF serial numbers 48-0608 to 48-0617 and had the constructor's numbers 2600-2609.

The first aircraft (VC-121B 48-0608) flew on 11 October 1948 and was delivered on 12 November. The remainder were delivered between then and March 1949 in the following variants:

C-121A: Six of the USAF order (48-0609, 0612, 0614, 0615, 0616 and 0617) were completed to basic C-121A standards with alternate layouts for 44 seated passengers, 20 casualty litters or freight. All were fitted with a 9ft 4in x 6ft 0in (2.74 x 1.83m) upwards hinging cargo door on the port side rear fuselage and a reinforced cabin floor. Power was provided by the same 2,500hp (1,864kW) Wright R-3350-C18-BD 18-cylinder radials as was fitted to the commercial models and the L.749A's maximum takeoff weight of 107,000lb (48,535kg) was retained.

Delivered from December 1948 and operated by the USAF Military Air Transport Service (MATS), some of the C-121As were used on trans-Atlantic operations supporting the Berlin Airlift of 1948-49, logging five million statute miles (8.05 million kilometres) of travel in the process.

48-0614 was used by General Dwight D Eisenhower as *Columbine I* when he was NATO Commander, it and three others subsequently converted to VC-121B standards (see below). All were withdrawn from service in 1967-68.

VC-121A: Three aircraft were completed to VC-121A VIP transport standards: 48-0611, 48-0610 *Columbine II* used by Eisenhower when he became US President in 1952, and 48-0613 *Bataan* used by General Douglas MacArthur.

Bataan was subsequently converted to a VC-121B and withdrawn from

The USAF received 10 Constellations based on the L.749. 48-0609 (c/n 2601) was a C-121A used by the Military Air Transport Service (MATS) and delivered in December 1948. Subsequent owners include movie star John Travolta.

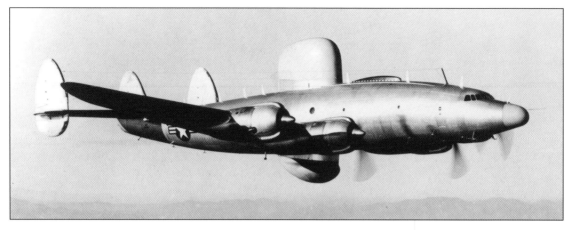

service in 1966, *Columbine II* was sold to Pan American in 1955, and 48-0611 was withdrawn from use in 1968 and later flown by several commercial operators.

VC-121B: The first of the USAF's new batch of Constellations (48-0608) was completed as a VC-121B for presidential transport with the planned name *Dewdrop* in anticipation of Thomas Dewey defeating the incumbent Harry Truman in the 1948 US presidential election.

It was delivered in November 1948 fitted with additional fuel tanks and a VVIP (very very important person) interior with accommodation for 24 day passengers or 10 berths and four sleeper seats.

Truman unexpectedly won the election and decided to retain his Douglas VC-118 (DC-6), 48-0608 instead being used by other high ranking government and Air Force officials before being downgraded to less opulent C-121B standards. It was retired in April 1968 and subsequently sold to Aircraft Specialities of Mesa, Arizona for conversion to a spray aircraft.

Four C-121As (48-0612, 0614, 0615 and 0617) were converted to VC-121Bs, as was VC-121A 48-0613.

PO-1W: Modified versions of the L.749A, the two PO-1Ws for the US Navy (BuAer 124437/38, c/n 2612/13) were built mainly to test the feasibility of carrying and operating large and powerful airborne early warning (AEW) radar systems. The concept was successful and more fully explored later with the development of Super Constellation AEW variants.

The basis of PO-1W was the installation of two large radomes, one above and one below the fuselage. The upper radome was 8ft (2.44) tall

Two PO-1W (later WV-1) airborne early warning aircraft were delivered to the US Navy in 1949-50 to test the feasibility of carrying and operating large radar systems. The concept was later fully exploited in the WV-2 based on the Super Constellation.

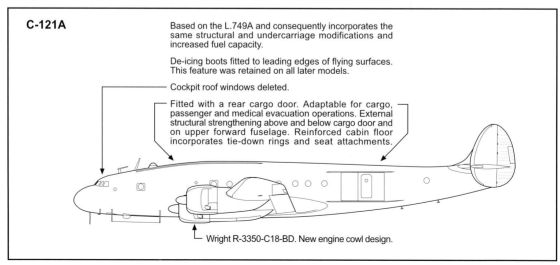

C-121A

Based on the L.749A and consequently incorporates the same structural and undercarriage modifications and increased fuel capacity.

De-icing boots fitted to leading edges of flying surfaces. This feature was retained on all later models.

Cockpit roof windows deleted.

Fitted with a rear cargo door. Adaptable for cargo, passenger and medical evacuation operations. External structural strengthening above and below cargo door and on upper forward fuselage. Reinforced cabin floor incorporates tie-down rings and seat attachments.

Wright R-3350-C18-BD. New engine cowl design.

VC-121A 48-0614
Columbine I (c/n 2606)
**was delivered to the
USAF as a VIP transport
in February 1949 and
later converted to a
VC-121B for VVIPs
including the US
President.**

and housed General Electric height finding radar, while the lower radome housed surveillance and distance measuring radar.

Larger outer vertical fins were installed to counter the directional instability caused by the radomes' greater side area, eight stub aerials were placed along the upper fuselage, weather radar was installed in the nose and a cargo door fitted to the port side rear fuselage.

Crew complement was up to 31, including flying and relief pilots, radar operators, technical and maintenance personnel. Bunks and a galley were installed in the cabin along with radar consoles and plotting tables.

The first PO-1W flew 9 June 1949 and the aircraft were delivered to the USN in August 1949 and April 1950. They were subsequently redesignated WV-1 and retired in 1957-58. Both were purchased by the US Federal Aviation Administration (FAA) with radar and other specialist equipment removed (carrying the civil registrations N119 and N120) before being transferred to the USAF in 1966.

The aircraft also carried civilian registration while in USAF service (N1192 and N1206) and were very briefly used for flights in areas where overtly US military aircraft might not be given airways clearance. Both were withdrawn later in 1966.

WV-1: The two PO-1Ws redesignated.

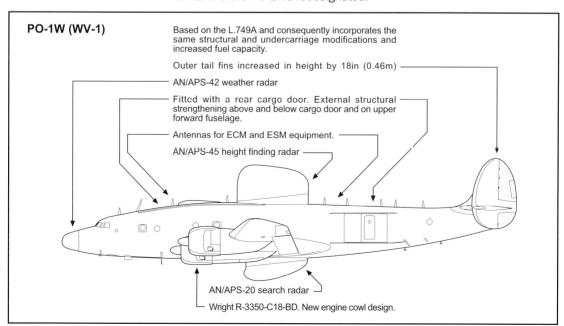

PO-1W (WV-1)

Based on the L.749A and consequently incorporates the same structural and undercarriage modifications and increased fuel capacity.

Outer tail fins increased in height by 18in (0.46m)

AN/APS-42 weather radar

Fitted with a rear cargo door. External structural strengthening above and below cargo door and on upper forward fuselage.

Antennas for ECM and ESM equipment.

AN/APS-45 height finding radar

AN/APS-20 search radar

Wright R-3350-C18-BD. New engine cowl design.

L.1049 Super Constellation

The he need for increased passenger capacity to cope with post war growth in air travel, greater range and better operating economics through lower seat-mile costs led to development of the stretched L.1049 Super Constellation series, the most produced of the family with 259 commercial and 320 military models built.

Lockheed began looking at stretched versions of the Constellation as early as 1943, studies initially based around an aircraft with the fuselage lengthened by 13 feet (3.96m) and accommodating up to 82 passengers. The intervention of World War II brought these ideas to a temporary halt and it wasn't until 1948-49 that serious work on a larger Constellation began.

The L.949 was the first concept to emerge, this combining an 11ft 10in (3.60m) fuselage stretch with 3,250hp (2,423kW) Wright R-3350 Turbo Compound engines, increased weights and accommodation for 70 passengers. An all cargo version called the 'Speedfreighter' was also envisaged.

Higher maximum takeoff weights were obviously an integral part of any stretched Constellation project and were tested during this period when an L.749 was successfully flown at a gross weight of 137,000lb (62,143kg), a substantial 30,000lb (13,608kg) heavier than standard.

The L.949 project gave way to the L.1049 Super Constellation later in 1949, this substantially revised design featuring an 18ft 4⌡in (5.60m) longer fuselage made up of two constant diameter 'plugs', the section forward of the front wing spar 10ft 8⌡in (3.27m) long and the rear section 7ft 8in (2.33m) in length. This allowed an increase in capacity to typically 69 first class passengers on international services and up to 95 in a high density configuration. A trans-continental sleeper variant was also made available with eight berths and 55 first class seats.

Other changes among the L.1049's 550 design revisions included replacement of the previous circular cabin windows with larger rectangular units (non transport military versions retained circular windows), installation of a 730 USgal (2,763 l) wing centre section fuel tank which increased total capacity to 6,550 USgal (24,794 l), and a substantially revised cockpit

The stretched Super Constellation provided the airlines with the greater seating capacity and lower seat-mile costs they needed as the air travel market expanded. N6901C (c/n 4015) is a standard L.1049, one of the first of 43 Super Constellations purchased new by TWA.

area in which a new seven (rather than nine) pane windscreen was mounted 3° inches (8.9cm) higher than before. A raised cockpit roof provided the pilots with an extra 7in (17.8cm) of headroom and the roofline over the cockpit took on a different, slightly flattened appearance.

The L.1049 also featured 18in (46cm) taller outboard vertical tail surfaces, similar to those installed on the US Navy's PO-1W airborne early warning aircraft based on the L.749A. Various structural and undercarriage strengthening measures were added to allow increased weights and the wing construction method was changed to incorporate large skin panels milled out of single metal pieces. This reduced weight and manufacturing complexity. The ailerons now had metal rather than fabric skinning.

Inside, the cabin environment was further improved with upgraded heating and ventilation systems while the pressurisation system was also boosted to provide an 8,000ft cabin altitude when the aircraft was flying at 22,800ft. On previous models, this cabin height was available to only 20,000ft.

The more powerful Wright R-3350 Turbo Compound engine with its exhaust driven power recovery turbines was planned for use on the Super Constellation from the start but its early non-availability meant that the original L.1049 for the airlines was powered by R-3350-C18 Cyclones producing 2,500hp (1,864kW) for takeoff and featuring conventional two-speed superchargers. The 30 per cent more powerful Turbo Compound would first appear on the L.1049C in 1953.

'Old 1961' Reborn

In order to expedite development of the Super Constellation, Lockheed decided not to built a new prototype from scratch but to convert the original Model 049 prototype which had first flown in February 1943.

The aircraft (nicknamed 'Old 1961' after its constructor's number) had in 1945 been converted to XC-69E configuration with 2,400hp (1,566kW) Pratt & Whitney R-2800-83 Double Wasp 18-cylinder radial engines, and in that form had been sold to industrialist (and TWA major shareholder) Howard Hughes in August 1946.

Lockheed repurchased the aircraft in May 1950 and over the northern summer of that year set about converting it to Super Constellation configuration, no mean feat considering the aircraft's curved and complex fuselage design. It was only a partial conversion, however, 'Old 1961' receiving the fuselage plugs but retaining its original circular cabin windows, cockpit/windscreen layout, short outer fins, structural specification and Pratt & Whitney Double Wasps.

Redesignated Model 049S (for 'Stretch'), given the revised constructor's

'Old 1961' - the original Constellation prototype - was purchased from Howard Hughes in 1950 and rebuilt as the first Super Constellation. It first flew in its new guise on 13 October 1950.

L.049/C-69 Constellation prototype NX25600/43-10309 (c/n 1961), first flight 9 January 1943.

L.049 Constellation NC90922 *Flagship Copenhagen* (c/n 2052), American Overseas Airlines 1948.

L.749 Constellation VH-EAA *Ross Smith* (c/n 2562), Qantas; converted to L.749A.

C-121A Constellation 48-0612 (c/n2604), USAF Military Air Transport Service 1949.

L.1049 Super Constellation N6902C *Star of the Seine* **(c/n 4016), TWA; collided with DC-7 over Grand Canyon June 1956.**

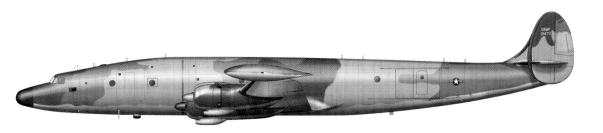

EC-121R Constellation 67-21477 (c/n 4444) USAF; ex USN WV-2 BuAer 141320.

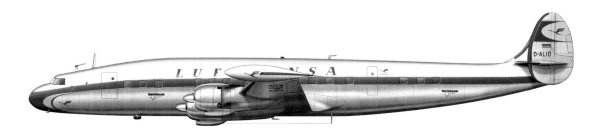

L.1049 Super Constellation D-ALID (c/n4647), Lufthansa, delivered August 1956.

L.1649A Starliner N7316C (c/n 1018), Alaska Airlines 1962-68; ex TWA *Star of the Tigris.*

number 1961S and carrying the new registration N6700, the rebuilt prototype first flew in its new guise on 13 October 1950, resplendent in a spectacular red, white and blue colour scheme.

'Old 1961' carried on Super Constellation testing alone until the first true L.1049 flew in July 1951. Before then, the aircraft had been grounded for further modification including installation in the number four (starboard outer) position of a Wright R-3350 CA-series engine which would power early production aircraft. The larger outboard fins and raised cockpit windows and roofline were also incorporated.

Type Certification of the L.1049 was awarded on 29 November 1951, 'Old 1961' subsequently used for more tests and trials of equipment which would later appear on both commercial and military Connies.

These included various Turbo Compound engine models (installed in numbers one and four positions), Hamilton Standard and Curtiss Electric propellers, tip tanks and the large dorsal and ventral fibreglass radomes used on early warning variants.

'Old 1961' was also used for troubleshooting including sorting out ongoing reliability problems with the Turbo Compound's power recovery turbines, testing different shaped engine cowlings to solve an overheating problem with the nacelles and adjacent wing skin area, and finding a cure for excessive exhaust flaming from the Turbo Compound. This flame sometimes spread all the way across the wing and out past the trailing edge, something which passengers not surprisingly found disconcerting. A revised exhaust stub shape and adjusted fuel pump timing solved the problem.

An early Allison YT-56 turboprop (as used on the C-130 Hercules military transport) was fitted to the number four position in April 1954, the aircraft performing much of the flight development work on this engine during 1954 and 1955.

The commercial version of the T56 - the Allison 501 - was installed in November 1956, again in the number four position and driving the four bladed, broad chord Aeroproducts propeller which would be fitted to the Electra.

'Old 1961' was finally withdrawn from use at the end of 1957 after an eventful career spanning nearly 15 years. Stored at Burbank, it was sold

The first true Super Constellation, L.1049 N6201C (c/n 4001), first flown on 14 July 1951 and later delivered to launch customer Eastern Air Lines. Eastern inaugurated Super Constellation services in December 1951.

to California Airmotive in December 1958 and partially broken up for spares before languishing unwanted as a prelude to being fully scrapped.

L.1049: The initial production version of the Super Constellation was very much a compromise, and although it had the main physical features described above, it lacked the planned Turbo Compound engines due to their unavailability. Military procurement of the engine was deemed more important than application to a civilian aircraft with the result that early production of the engine was allocated to the Douglas Skyraider naval strike and Lockheed Neptune maritime patrol aircraft.

As a result, the L.1049 was regarded as underpowered with its 2,500hp (1,864kW) conventionally supercharged R-3350-C Cyclones and maximum takeoff weight of 120,000lb (54,432kg).

The first true L.1049 Super Constellation (N6201C, c/n 4001) flew on 14 July 1951 and deliveries of the new model to launch customer Eastern Air Lines began the following November. Services were inaugurated on 7 December 1951 on the New York-Miami route.

Eastern had ordered 10 L.1049s in April 1950 and subsequently increased this to 14. Its aircraft lacked the centre section fuel tank and were therefore used exclusively on domestic routes. Deliveries to Eastern were completed in April 1952 and the survivors were withdrawn from service in 1967-68.

The only other L.1049 customer was TWA, which ordered 10 in December 1950. Like Eastern, TWA chose not to fit the centre section fuel tank to its aircraft and therefore used them for domestic services. Deliveries began in May 1952 and had been completed five months later. TWA didn't keep its L.1049s for very long, starting to dispose of them as early as 1960.

The L.1049s were all upgraded with 2,700hp (2,013kW) R-3350-C18-CA1 engines in 1953 but this only slightly helped the performance problems. TWA incorporated some modifications in an attempt to reduce drag and extract a bit more speed out of aircraft, including to the engine nacelles and propeller spinners, blocking off one of the three cabin cooling intakes on the wings and even removing the wing walkway paint! The result was a 10kt (18km/h) speed increase at cruising altitude.

TWA L.1049s were involved in two of the USA's worst air disasters. On 30 June 1956 N6902C (c/n 4016) *Star of the Seine* and a United Air

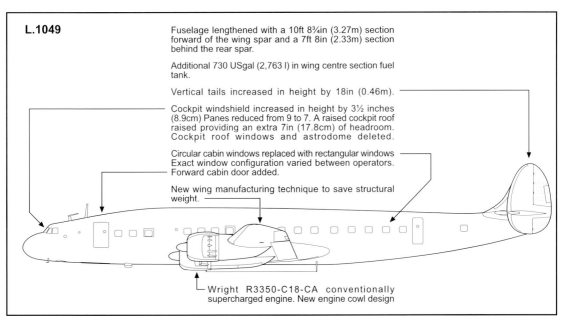

L.1049

Fuselage lengthened with a 10ft 8¾in (3.27m) section forward of the wing spar and a 7ft 8in (2.33m) section behind the rear spar.

Additional 730 USgal (2,763 l) in wing centre section fuel tank.

Vertical tails increased in height by 18in (0.46m).

Cockpit windshield increased in height by 3½ inches (8.9cm) Panes reduced from 9 to 7. A raised cockpit roof raised providing an extra 7in (17.8cm) of headroom. Cockpit roof windows and astrodome deleted.

Circular cabin windows replaced with rectangular windows Exact window configuration varied between operators. Forward cabin door added.

New wing manufacturing technique to save structural weight.

Wright R3350-C18-CA conventionally supercharged engine. New engine cowl design

Lines Douglas DC-7 collided over the Grand Canyon in clear weather, killing all on board both aircraft.

The accident resulted in a shakeup of US air traffic control procedures when it was revealed that although controllers knew the two aircraft were at the same altitude and on intersecting tracks, the fact they were flying outside controlled airspace meant there was no obligation to inform the flight crews of the conflict in a 'see and be seen' situation.... so they didn't.

On 16 December 1960 L.1049 N6907C (c/n 4021) *Star of Sicily* and a United Air Lines Douglas DC-8 collided over Brooklyn, New York. Once again all on board died and the damage on the ground was substantial.

Subsequent operators of ex Eastern and TWA L.1049s included the Happy Hours Travel Club, Aerotours Dominicanas, Modern Air Transport, Standard Airways, Aeronaves del Panama and California Hawaiian Airlines.

L.1049B: Lockheed designation for some US Air Force and US Navy military Super Constellation variants (see next chapter).

L.1049C: The potential of the Super Constellation as a significant airliner on international routes was able to be better realised with the L.1049C, the first model powered by Wright Turbo Compound engines.

The R-3350-TC18-DA1 engines delivered 3,250hp (2,423kW) for takeoff, this 30 per cent increase over the original L.1049's powerplants allowing an increase in maximum takeoff weight to 133,000lb (60,329kg) which in turn permitted use of the centre section fuel tank which had not been fitted to the L.1049. The result was a much improved aircraft with higher speeds and substantially better payload-range performance.

Early versions of the R-3350 produced up to 2,700hp (2,013kW) utilising conventional two-speed gear driven superchargers. The Turbo Compound engines' two-speed superchargers were 'compounded' by three 'blow down' exhaust gas power recovery turbines mounted on the rear section of the crankcase. Each had quill driveshafts transmitting power from the turbines to an extension of the crankshaft. The exhaust pipes from six adjacent engine cylinders were connected to each turbine intake, the gasses from these feeding back to the engine and producing an extra 550hp (410kW).

The Turbo Compound retained the basic characteristics of earlier R-3350s: 18-cylinder two row radial, cylinder bore 6.125in (155mm), piston stroke 6.3125in (160mm), displacement 3,347cu in (54.9 litres), maximum revolutions 2,900rpm and the use of 115/145 octane fuel. Compression ratio was 6.7:1 and specific fuel consumption at cruise power 0.38lb/hp/hr, a 12 per cent improvement over the previous engine.

The DA-series engine used in the L.1049C and subsequent Super Constellations produced 3,250hp (2,423kW) for takeoff at 2,900rpm,

The L.1049C was the first civil version powered by Wright Turbo Compound engines, these complex and temperamental powerplants producing much greater outputs than the standard R-3350. World Wide Airways' CF-RNR (c/n 4544) started life in 1954 as an L.1049C with Trans-Canada Airlines and was later upgraded to an E and finally a G with tip tanks.

2,650hp (1,976kW) at 6,500ft and 2,600rpm, and 2,450hp (1,827kW) at 17,900ft and 2,600rpm.

The advanced and complex Turbo Compound provided the power required for the Super Constellation but was also subject to a high unreliability due mainly to problems with the power recovery turbines and associated systems. Three engined arrivals were common, and the Turbo Compound powered Super Constellations quickly earned the nickname 'The World's Best Trimotor'. The similarly powered Douglas DC-7 also suffered.

The first L.1049C (PH-TFP, c/n 4501 for KLM Royal Dutch Airlines) flew on 17 February 1953, three months before the directly competitive DC-7. KLM put its first aircraft into service in August 1953 on the Amsterdam-New York route, this event also three months before the DC-7's inaugural service.

At this stage the Lockheed aircraft held the advantage over the Douglas product due to its superior payload-range, prompting Douglas to quickly develop the longer range DC-7B (which still needed a fuel stop flying east to west across the Atlantic against the prevailing wind) and then the definitive Douglas piston engined airliner, the DC-7C 'Seven Seas'.

L.1049C production amounted to 49 aircraft for KLM (9), Eastern (16), Air France (10), Trans-Canada (5), Qantas (4), Pakistan International (3) and Air India (2). The last of the model was VH-EAJ *Southern Star* (c/n 4549) for Qantas, delivered in June 1954.

Air France later converted nine of its L.1049Cs to L.1049E and then L.1049G standards, Trans-Canada did the same with its five aircraft and all four of the Qantas Cs were modified to E models.

L.1049D: Based on the US Navy's R7V-1 (L.1049B) transport and incorporating features of the L.1049C airliner, four L.1049D convertertible freighters were built for Seaboard & Western Airlines (Seaboard World from 1961). They were delivered in August and September 1954 carrying the registrations N6501C-N6504C and constructor's numbers 4163-4166, these within the R7V-1 sequence.

The L.1049D featured a reduced number of rectangular cabin windows, large freight doors front and rear and a heavy duty floor made from magnesium planks incorporating tie down rings and seat attachment points. The cabin

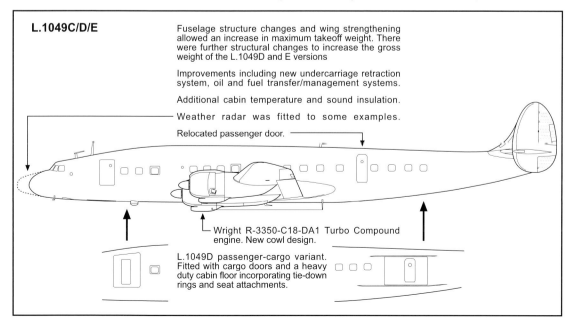

L.1049C/D/E

Fuselage structure changes and wing strengthening allowed an increase in maximum takeoff weight. There were further structural changes to increase the gross weight of the L.1049D and E versions

Improvements including new undercarriage retraction system, oil and fuel transfer/management systems.

Additional cabin temperature and sound insulation.

Weather radar was fitted to some examples.

Relocated passenger door.

Wright R-3350-C18-DA1 Turbo Compound engine. New cowl design.

L.1049D passenger-cargo variant. Fitted with cargo doors and a heavy duty cabin floor incorporating tie-down rings and seat attachments.

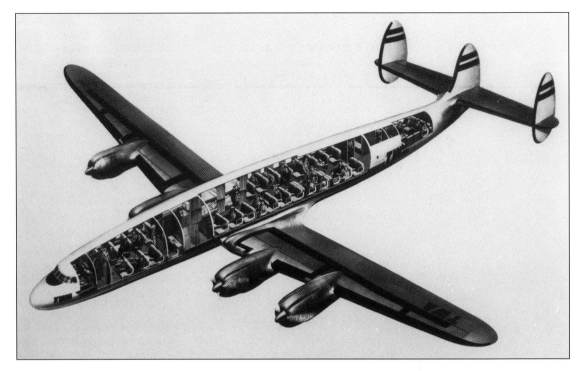

could be converted to accommodate up to 109 passengers in a high density layout.

Powerplants were the same 3,250hp (2,423kW) Turbo Compounds as fitted to the L.1049C, maximum takeoff weight remained at 133,000lb (60,329kg) and a maximum payload of 38,750lb (17,577kg) could be carried.

All four L.1049Ds were leased to BOAC for various periods between 1954 and 1956 before returning to Seaboard & Western. One crashed on takeoff at New York's Idlewild Airport in November 1958. The others were converted to L.1049H standards for further service with Seaboard before being passed on to new owners.

L.1049E: Similar to the L.1049C but with some structural strengthening to allow an increase in maximum takeoff weight to 135,400lb (61,417kg). Eight airlines took delivery of 25 L.1049Es: Air India (3), Avianca (3), Cubana (1), Iberia (3), KLM (4), Linea Aeropostal Venezolana (2), Qantas (6) and Trans-Canada (3). The first aircraft was EC-AIN (c/n 4550) delivered to Iberia on 4 June 1954 and the last (VT-DHN, c/n 4615) was handed over to Air India in February 1955.

Air India, Iberia, KLM, Tans-Canada, LAV and Qantas between them had 16 L.1049Es subsequently converted to L.1049G standards, while 18 L.1049Cs were converted to Es.

L.1049F: Lockheed designation for the US Air Force's C-121C transport (see next chapter).

L.1049G: In October 1954 Douglas flew the first example of its DC-7B with additional fuel capacity and about 400nm (740km) more range with a typical payload, this still not quite sufficient to cross the Atlantic east-west against the prevailing wind most of the time.

While the DC-7B was being developed, Lockheed was also working on a longer range Super Constellation which matched the range of the DC-7B but suffered the same operational limitations as the Douglas aircraft across the Atlantic. It did, however have superior range to the DC-7B when carrying a heavy payload.

A Lockheed cutaway drawing showing the interior arrangement of a TWA Super Constellation with first class seats four abreast, some sleeping berths and rear lounge.

For Douglas, the DC-7B was an interim international model pending the introduction of the substantially revised and considerably longer ranging DC-7C 'Seven Seas' a year later. The DC-7C outperformed the new L.1049G Super Constellation in terms of range, forcing Lockheed to develop the last of the line, the rewinged and very long range L.1649 Starliner, as described in a later chapter. This went into service nearly a year behind the DC-7C and as a result sold only modestly at the very end of the age of piston engined airliners.

It's interesting to compare the sales performances of the DC-7 and directly competitive Super Constellation from the L.1049C onwards, both powered by the Wright Turbo Compound engine.

Excluding military sales (of which there were none for the DC-7 models), production of the basic DC-7 reached 105, followed by 112 DC-7Bs and 121 DC-7Cs for a total of 338. There were 49 L.1049C Super Constellations built plus four L.1049Ds, 25 L.1049Es, 104 L.1049Gs and 53 L.1049Hs (total 235) plus 44 Starliners, bringing the overall total up to 279.

The L.1049G Super Constellation featured several improvements over its immediate predecessors including more reliable R-3350-TC18-DA3 Turbo Compound engines with the same 3,250hp (2,423kW) power rating as before, revised de-icing equipment for the wings and tailplane and a further increased maximum takeoff weight of 137,500lb (62,370kg) as a result of more structural strengthening.

Further attempts were made to improve noise and vibration levels in the cabin by installing new soundproofing material in the cabin walls and developing more efficient rubber shock pads for the engine mountings. RCA AVQ-10 weather radar could also be fitted in a nosecone lengthened by 2ft 7in (79cm), this option also made available for some earlier models.

The most important new feature of the L.1049G was its increased fuel capacity, achieved by a pair of optional 600 USgal (2,271 l) tip tanks, these bringing the maximum fuel load up to 7,750 USgal (29,337 l). The tip tanks had first been introduced to Constellation production during 1954 on the US Navy's WV-2 early warning aircraft and the USAF's similar RC-121D.

The first L.1049G (N5173V, c/n 4575 for Northwest) flew on 17 December 1954 and was delivered on 22 January 1955, reversing the two month advantage held by the DC-7B on first flight date and beating it into service by four months. The L.1049G went on to become the best selling of all commercial Constellations with 104 built for 16 airlines and one corporate customer. The last example (VT-DJX, c/n 4687) was handed over to Air India in August 1958.

Operators taking delivery of new L.1049Gs were Air India (5), Air France (14),

Air India was a major Super Constellation operator, taking delivery of two L.1049Cs, three L.1049Es and five L.1049Gs. The Es were upgraded to L.1049G standards.

Avianca (1), Cubana (3), Eastern (10), Hughes Tool Co (2), Iberia (2), KLM (6), LAV (2), Lufthansa (8), Northwest (4), Qantas (4), Thai Airways (3), Trans-Canada (4), Transportes Aereas Portugueses (3), TWA (27) and Varig (6). TWA marketed its new aircraft as the 'Super G', the fact proclaimed by painting a large 'G' on their outer fins.

Of the two L.1049Gs delivered to the Hughes Tool Co (c/n 4619 delivered February 1956) remained in storage at Burbank until January 1960 when it was repurchased by Lockheed and immediately sold on to Capitol Airways. The second Hughes aircraft (c/n 4648 delivered May 1956) was leased out to TWA the following month.

Even though the L.1049G was still not capable of crossing the Atlantic east-west non stop on a routine basis, its extra range and increased weights did give operators the chance to introduce new services in other parts of the world and to carry greater payloads on existing routes.

Australia's Qantas was able to put the additional payload-range performance to good use on its Pacific and other routes and created a bit of history with the L.1049G in 1958 when it launched what was claimed to be the world's first around-the-world scheduled services. Eleven years earlier, Pan American had made a similar claim when it inaugurated a service from New York to New York (via 17 stages) using an L.049.

Qantas launched its around-the-world service on 14 January 1958 from Melbourne using two L.1049Gs, one travelling eastbound through Fiji, Honolulu, San Francisco and New York before returning to Australia, and the other flying west through Jakarta, Singapore, Bangkok, Calcutta, Karachi, Bahrein, Athens and Rome. Both arrived back in Australia on 20 January.

These flights set the scene for two complete around-the-world services each week, one from Sydney and the other from Melbourne. The aircraft involved in the inaugural flights were VH-EAO *Southern Aurora* (c/n 4679) and VH-EAP *Southern Zephyr* (c/n 4680) which had been delivered in October and November 1957, respectively.

L.1049H: The final Super Constellation version, the L.1049H was a convertible passenger/freight aircraft. It combined the basic mechanical specification of the L.1049G with the L.1049D's cargo carrying capabilities including the strengthened floor with tie down rings and seat attachment points and large freight doors.

The L.1049H's maximum zero fuel weight (above which all load must be fuel) was substantially increased to provide a maximum payload of more than 40,000lb (18,145kg), which could be carried over a range of 1,640nm (3,037km).

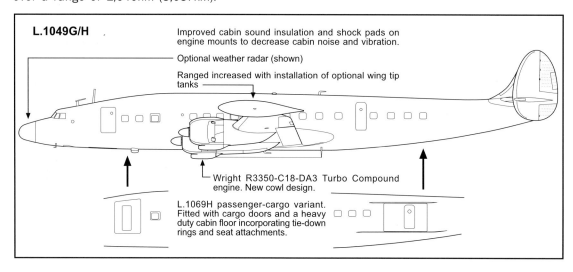

L.1049G/H

Improved cabin sound insulation and shock pads on engine mounts to decrease cabin noise and vibration.

Optional weather radar (shown)

Ranged increased with installation of optional wing tip tanks

Wright R3350-C18-DA3 Turbo Compound engine. New cowl design.

L.1069H passenger-cargo variant. Fitted with cargo doors and a heavy duty cabin floor incorporating tie-down rings and seat attachments.

Qantas L.1049C VH-EAG Southern Constellation (c/n 4539) delivered in March 1954. This aircraft was later converted to an E.

A TWA 'Super G' over the Statue of Liberty. The L.1049G introduced optional tip tanks and radar to the Constellation, both of which are fitted to this aircraft.

Conversion from freight to passenger configuration or vice-versa could be achieved in a few hours by the use of quickly removable interior furnishings such as toilets, galleys, baggage racks, interior lining panels and seats. As a passenger aircraft, the L.1049H could accommodate up to 94 people.

The first L.1049H (c/n 4801) flew on 20 September 1956 and was delivered to launch customer Qantas the following month as VH-EAM *Southern Spray*. A total of 53 was built, delivered to Qantas (2), Seaboard & Western (5), Flying Tiger Line (13), California Eastern Aviation (5), Air Finance Corporation (3), Resort Airlines (2), Dollar Associates (1), National Airlines (4), REAL SA (4), Pakistan International (2), TWA (6), KLM (3), Slick Airways (1) and Trans-Canada Airlines (2).

The aircraft delivered to California Eastern, Air Finance Corp, Resort Airlines and Dollar Associates were immediately leased out to other operators, TWA taking an additional five and Flying Tiger two in this manner.

Transcontinental leased two from California Eastern and Transocean received one each from Dollar and Air Finance Corp. The L.1049H's quick change characteristics and enhanced payload capability made it suitable for supplemental and charter operators such as Slick, Seaboard & Western and Flying Tiger.

An upgrade to the L.1049H's specification was made available shortly after deliveries began, this incorporating the more powerful 3,400hp (2,535kW) R-3350-TC18-EA2 Turbo Compound engines as installed in the L.1649A Starliner and an increased maximum takeoff weight of 140,000lb (63,504kg) to further improve payload-range performance.

L.1049H production was completed towards the end of 1958, ending the Constellation/Super Constellation/Starliner manufacturing story after nearly 16 years. The last production aircraft (c/n 4853) was delivered to Flying Tiger in late September 1958 but the operator took delivery of c/n 4852 in October while Trans-Canada Airlines received c/nos 4850 and 4851 in December 1958 and January 1959, respectively.

One L.1049H (c/n 4849) remained unsold at the start of 1959, this from a cancelled TWA order. After a period of storage the aircraft was handed over to Slick Airways as N6936C on 7 August 1959 as the final delivery of any new Constellation.

LAS Cargo Conversion: Lockheed's maintenance and modification subsidiary, Lockheed Air Services, offered cargo conversions for L.749s, L.1049s and L.1649s. Its basis was the installation of a cargo floor plus port side forward and aft freight doors similar to those on the L.1049D and H models.

The forward door was 4ft 8½in (1.43m) wide and 6ft 0in (1.83m) high; the rear unit measured 8ft 10½in x 6ft 0in (2.70m x 1.83m). Super Constellation conversions were performed for Eastern Air Lines, Qantas and Skyways of London, while Lufthansa had two Starliners

Lufthansa L.1049G D-ALAK (c/n 4602), the first of eight ordered by the airline and delivered in March 1955. This aircraft has tip tanks but lacks radar.

The L.1049H Super Constellation was a convertible passenger/freight model with large cargo doors, strengthened cabin floor and revised operating weights. PP-YSA (c/n 4834) of Brazil's REAL SA was delivered in early 1958, the final year of Constellation production.

converted and TWA eight.

L.1149: Proposal to re-engine L.1049G Super Constellations with 3,750shp (2,796kW) Allison 501 turboprops as fitted to the Lockheed Electra. Not built.

L.1249: Two R7V-2s (US Navy) and two YC-121Fs (USAF) tested with Pratt & Whitney T34 turboprops (see next chapter).

L.1449: Proposal for L.1049G stretched by 4ft 7in (1.40m), fitted with a new wing (as later applied to the Starliner) and Pratt & Whitney PT2F-1 or Rolls-Royce Tyne turboprops; not built.

L.1549: Proposal for further stretched (by 7ft 11in/2.41m) variant of L.1449. Not built.

The manufacture of the last Super Constellations in the second half of 1958 coincided with the arrival of the Boeing 707, Pan American putting the new jet into service in October. The Douglas DC-8 entered service a year later and a new age in commercial air transport had arrived.

Most major airlines had replaced their Constellations with 707s or DC-8s on mainline international services by the early 1960s, although some retained small fleets as freighters or backup aircraft until the jets completely took over.

TWA, for example, operated its last L.1049 trans-Atlantic service in August 1961 and kept the type on domestic flights for two more years. TWA's last L.1049G was retired in early 1967 but remarkably, the final L.749 passenger flight wasn't until April 1967. An L.1049G freighter operated TWA's ultimate Constellation service the following month.

Constellations continued to fly for many years with their second, third, fourth or even fifth owners, often as freighters and as the years progressed with small operators in Africa or the Americas. By the early 1990s only a

handful remained in commercial service in Central America but these gradually faded away over the next few years.

One notable exception to the early retirement of Constellations by a major US airline was Eastern. In April 1961 the airline launched its Air Shuttle service linking New York, Boston and Washington DC.

The concept was simple - this was an aerial no reservations 'bus service' where passengers would simply turn up for the hourly departures, pay the discounted fare and get on an aircraft. A seat was guaranteed, so if there was one passenger too many for the available seating, another aircraft would be rolled out to accommodate him or her.

Eastern initially used eight L.1049Cs configured to seat 95 passengers on the Air Shuttle but the popularity of the service was such that within two years all of the airline's remaining 32 L.1049s, L.1049Cs and L.1049Gs were pressed into service. The Air Shuttle lasted until February 1968, by which time the small number of Constellations still in Eastern's fleet were used only for backup, but the exercise represented an interesting and unexpected swansong for the aircraft in US regular airline service.

Qantas took delivery of 20 new production Constellations in five versions over the years as well as second hand aircraft. VH-EAM *Southern Spray* (c/n 4801) was the first L.1049H off the line, delivered in October 1956.

L.1049 SUPER CONSTELLATION

Powerplants: L.1049 - four 2,500hp (1,864kW) Wright R-3350-C18BD1 or 2,700hp (2,013kW) R-3350-C18-CA1 Cyclone 18-cylinder radials; Hamilton-Standard or Curtiss Electric three bladed propellers of 15ft 2in (4.62m) diameter. Max fuel capacity 6,550 USgal (24,794 l) in wing and centre section tanks.

L.1049C/E - four 3,250hp (2,423kW) Wright R-3350-TC18-DA1 Turbo Compound 18-cylinder radials. Fuel capacity 6,550 USgal (24,794 l).

L.1049G - four 3,250hp (2,523kW) R-3350-TC18-DA3 Turbo Compounds. Max fuel capacity 7,750 USgal (29,337 l) with optional 600 USgal (2,271 l) tip tanks.

Dimensions: Wing span 123ft 0in (37.49m) or 123ft 5in (37.62m) with tip tanks; length 113ft 7in (34.62m) or 116ft 2in (35.41m) with radar nose; height 24ft 9in (7.54m); wing area 1,650sq ft (153.3m^2).

Weights: L.1049 - empty 69,000lb (31,298kg); max takeoff 120,000lb (54,432kg); max landing 101,500lb (46,040kg); max payload 19,335lb (8,770kg).

L.1049C - empty 70,083lb (31,790kg); max takeoff 133,000lb (60,329kg); max landing 110,000lb (49,896kg); max payload 26,400lb (11,975kg).

L.1049E - max takeoff 135,400lb (61,417kg).

L.1049G - empty 73,016lb (33,120kg); max takeoff 137,500lb (62,370kg); max landing 113,000lb (51,256kg); max payload 24,293lb (11,019kg).

Accommodation: Typically 69 passengers on international routes or up to 95 passengers in high density arrangement; sleeper arrangement for typically eight berths and 55 first class seats. Cabin length 83ft 2in (25.35m); height 6ft 6in (1.98m); max width 10ft 8.6in (3.26m). Underfloor freight/luggage capacity 728cu ft (20.6m^3) in two holds.

Performance: L.1049 - normal cruise 261kt (484km/h); service ceiling 25,700ft; max payload range 2,268nm (4,200km).

L.1049C - max speed 325kt (602km/h); normal cruise 273kt (505km/h); service ceiling 23,200ft; max payload range 2,500nm (4,630km); max range 4,136nm (7,660km).

L.1049E - max speed 327kt (604km/h) at 20,000ft; max cruise 287kt (532km/h) at 23,000ft; initial climb 1,140ft (347m)/min; max range 4,188nm (7,757km).

L.1049G - max speed 318kt (589km/h); normal cruise 270kt (500km/h); service ceiling 22,800ft; range with 18,300lb (8,300kg) payload 3,600nm (6,668km); range with 8,500lb (3,855kg) payload 4,562nm (8,450km).

(Opposite) The L.1049H found favour with US supplemental and freight carriers such as Slick Airways. N6936C (c/n 4849) was the last new Constellation delivered, handed over to Slick in September 1959 after a period of storage.

Military Supers

A very large part of the sales success of the Constellation family was its acceptance in substantial numbers by the US military. As has been noted earlier, of the 233 Constellations, 579 Super Constellations and 44 Starliners built, 346 or more than 40 per cent of the total production run went to the American Services.

Three hundred and twenty of these were L.1049 variants, this figure representing some 55 per cent of the Super Constellation production total of 579. From these figures it can be seen that procurement of the aircraft by the US Air Force and Navy made a substantial contribution to the success of the programme. It also added about 40 variants and subvariants to the list of models, these fulfilling a variety of roles.

US Navy

The US Navy was the single largest customer for the Constellation, receiving a total of 204 aircraft. The service's association with the aircraft began in August 1949 with the delivery of the first of two PO-1W airborne early warning (AEW) testbeds (see earlier chapter), these proving the feasibility of the concept and resulting in its further development using the Super Constellation airframe.

AEW was one of the two primary roles for which the US Navy used its Super Constellations, these initially designated WV and officially named Warning Star. The other major role was transport under the designation R7V. Both versions and their variants were redesignated in the C-121 series from September 1962 when US Navy and Marine Corps designations were integrated with the existing USAF system.

R7V-1: The first Super Constellation variant to enter US military service, the R7V-1 transport was also the first to be delivered with Wright Turbo Compound engines, preceding the similarly powered commercial L.1049C into service by seven months.

Carrying the company designation L.1049B, the R7V-1 was powered by four 3,250hp (2,423kW) R-3350-91 Turbo Compounds. It featured a reinforced cabin floor for the carriage of freight, large cargo doors, a small number of circular cabin windows (commercial Super Constellations had more numerous rectangular windows) and accommodation for up to 106 passengers in backwards facing and removable seats. Alternative loads of 73 stretcher casualties or up to 41,885lb (19,000kg) of freight could be carried.

The R7V-1 also introduced weather radar mounted in a lengthened nose to the Constellation series. The fuel capacity and initial maximum

More WV-2 (later EC-121K) Warning Stars were built than any other Constellation variant with 142 delivered to the US Navy in 1954-58. BuAer 141309 (c/n 4433) was from the middle of the production run and was photographed here at Sydney in September 1968 carrying 'Pacific Missile Range' markings.

takeoff weight of 133,000lb (60,329kg) were the same as the L.1049C, the latter subsequently increasing to 135,400lb (61,417kg). Some were later fitted with the 600 USgal (2,271 l) tip tanks which appeared on the WV-2 Warning Star and L.1049G Super Constellation.

The first of 50 R7V-1s (BuAer 128434, c/n 4101) was handed over to the US Navy on 5 November 1952, the remaining aircraft following between then and July 1954. They were used primarily for the Navy's contribution to the Military Air Transport Service (MATS). Thirty-two were transferred to USAF control in June 1958 under the new designation C-121G and with new USAF serial numbers.

The US Navy's remaining R7V-1s were redesignated C-121J in September 1962.

R7V-1P: One aircraft fitted with cameras for survey work in the Antarctic; flown by Squadron VXE-6 in this role and carrying the name *Phoenix*.

R7V-2: In order for the US services to gain experience with turboprop engines and to evaluate them, four airframes were set aside for the installation of 5,700shp (4,250kW) Pratt & Whitney T34 powerplants. All four R7V-2s were intended for operation by the USN but the last two were transferred to the USAF as YC-121Fs upon completion.

The two USN R7V-2s carried the serials 131630 and 131631 (c/n 4131-4132), the first of them flying on 1 September 1953. They were handed over to the USN in December 1953 and January 1954, tests including high speed dives and overload operations up to a maximum weight of 166,400lb (75,480kg). Other modifications incorporated included the fitting of tip and additional wing fuel tanks, providing a maximum fuel capacity of 8,770 USgal (33,198 l).

R7V-2 performance figures included a maximum cruising speed of 382kt (708km/h), normal cruise 339kt (628km/h) at 26,500ft, and design range with reserves 2,605nm (4,825km) carrying a 20,000lb (9,072kg) payload. Normal maximum takeoff weight was 150,000lb (68,040kg).

The R7V-2 programme ended in late 1956, after which the second aircraft was loaned to Lockheed for the installation of 3,750shp (2,796kW) Allison 501D turboprops as part of the Electra airliner development programme. During this period it was named *Elation*, a happy combination of the Electra and Constellation names.

Turboprop testbed - one of two R7V-2s powered by Pratt & Whitney T34s evaluated by the US Navy for three years from late 1953. The USAF also flew a pair of them as the YC-121F.

WV-2 Warning Star: Originally designated PO-2W but renamed WV-2 by the time deliveries began in March 1954, the WV-2 Warning Star airborne early warning (AEW) and radar intelligence aircraft was the production follow-on to the pair of successful L.749 based PO-1W evaluation aircraft delivered to the USN in 1949-50.

The WV-2 used the Turbo Compound powered Super Constellation as its basis and was fitted with tip tanks. Its early warning radar and associated equipment weighed 13,000lb (5,900kg) and the aircraft operated at an increased maximum takeoff weight of 143,600lb (65,137kg).

Like the WV-1, the WV-2 featured large radomes above and below the fuselage, the upper unit housing General Electric APS-45 height finding radar and the lower radome APS-20 surveillance and distance measuring radar with a detection range of 200 miles (320km) at 25,000ft. AN/APS-42 weather radar was installed in the nose.

Inside, accommodation was provided for a crew of between 26 and 31 comprising flight crew, radar operators, technicians and maintenance specialists, some of whom were relief crews as mission endurances of 24 hours or more were possible. Bunks, hot meal galleys and a repair shop were provided.

Five radar consoles and plotting tables were installed, these allowing the observation of various presentations or segments of the same basic radar picture. This allowed operators and analysts to simultaneously work on several search and interception problems, enhanced by auxiliary radar units which provided specialised information. A Combat Information Centre (CIC) co-ordinated all search information for communication to ships, other aircraft or land bases, this supported by datalinks and other communications systems.

The aerodynamic configuration of the WV-2 was initially tested on the original Constellation prototype which had been rebuilt as the first Super

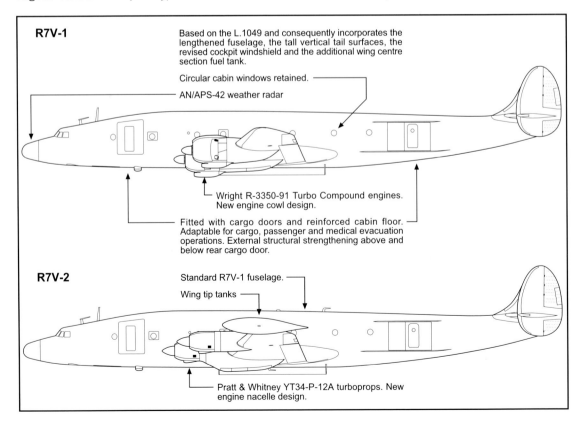

R7V-1

Based on the L.1049 and consequently incorporates the lengthened fuselage, the tall vertical tail surfaces, the revised cockpit windshield and the additional wing centre section fuel tank.

Circular cabin windows retained.

AN/APS-42 weather radar

Wright R-3350-91 Turbo Compound engines. New engine cowl design.

Fitted with cargo doors and reinforced cabin floor. Adaptable for cargo, passenger and medical evacuation operations. External structural strengthening above and below rear cargo door.

R7V-2

Standard R7V-1 fuselage.

Wing tip tanks

Pratt & Whitney YT34-P-12A turboprops. New engine nacelle design.

The sole WV-2E (later EC-121L), converted from the first WV-1 (BuAer 126512, c/n 4301) in 1956. The pylon mounted 'rotodome' dish containing surveillance radar later became the norm for airborne early warning (AEW) aircraft.

The Lockheed 'Elation', one of the R7V-2s fitted with four Allison 501 turboprops as part of the Electra airliner development programme.

Constellation in 1950. Fitted with dummy radomes and tip tanks, the aircraft was tested in WV-2 configuration in 1952.

The USN ordered WV-2s in July 1950 as part of an overall order for 244 Super Constellation variants, this later revised downwards. Production of the WV-2 amounted to 142 aircraft, the largest of any single Constellation model. Deliveries to the USN began in March 1954 and continued until October 1958.

Working in conjunction with the USAF's similar RC-121C and RC-121D AEW aircraft, the WV-2 provided extensive early warning coverage over the Atlantic and Pacific Oceans during the height of the Cold War period flying with USN squadrons VW-2, VW-3, VW-11 and VW-13. They operated in this role until August 1965, by which time the new designation EC-121K had been applied. Thirty-nine EC-121Ks were transferred to the USAF in two batches in 1962 and 1967.

WV-2E: The first WV-2 (BuAer 126512, c/n 4301) was converted to WV-2E configuration, this involving a pioneer installation of surveillance radar rotating in a large dish mounted above the fuselage on a substantial pylon.

The WV-2E's AN/APS-70 aerial surveillance radar was mounted in a 37ft (11.3m) diameter aerodynamically shaped dish (called a 'rotodome'), its supporting pylon also housing the WV-2's original APS-45 radar. The APS-20 radar and its ventral radome was removed. The new radar offered considerable enhancement over the WV-2's capabilities and was able to detect targets at up to three times the distance.

BuAer 126512 was originally delivered to the USN in October 1954 and made its first flight in WV-2E configuration on 8 August 1956. It was redesignated EC-121L in 1962 shortly before being withdrawn.

The WV-2E was intended meet a USN requirement at a time when turboprop versions of the Super Constellation were still being considered. In production form the aircraft would have been designated W2V-1 with turboprops, but the USN ordered the much smaller, carrier based Grumman W2F-1 (later E-2 Hawkeye) to meet its needs.

WV-2Q: Eight WV-2s converted for electronic countermeasures (ECM) duties. The aircraft involved were BuAer 131390-131392, 135747 , 131749, 131751-131752 and 143209; all redesignated EC-121M in 1962.

WV-3: Eight new production Warning Stars (BuAer 137891-137898, c/n 4378-4385) were completed as weather reconnaissance aircraft. A ninth aircraft (BuAer 141323, c/n 4447) was later converted from a WV-2.

The WV-3s were equipped with specialist air sampling and weather recording equipment plus other electronic data collection gear. A crew of up to 26 was carried including a number of scientists and meteorologists.

The WV-3s achieved some fame internationally when film footage taken from them while flying through the middle of hurricanes was shown on television and in cinemas, the nicknames 'Hurricane Hunter' and 'Storm Seeker' quickly applied.

Delivery of the eight new WV-3s to the USN took place in April 1956. BuAer 137891 was badly damaged while flying through a hurricane in August 1964 but landed safely, although the aircraft had to be scrapped afterwards. By then, the fleet had been redesignated WC-121N.

After further conversion to EC-121R standards as airborne relay stations for use in Vietnam, BuAer 137895 and 137898 were transferred to the USAF in early 1967 with the new serial numbers 67-21471/21472 and remained in service until 1971. The Navy's last WC-121N was withdrawn from use by squadron VW-4 in April 1972.

C-121J: September 1962 redesignation of R7V-1.

NC-121J: Airborne television and radio studios and transmitter aircraft converted from R7V-1/C-121Js by Lockheed Air Services for use in Vietnam. Three conversions were performed (BuAer 128444, 131627, 131641), the aircraft serving in Vietnam between 1967 and 1970.

The NC-121Js were known as 'Blue Eagles' and operated under the command of the US Navy Oceanographic Air Survey Unit. They were able to

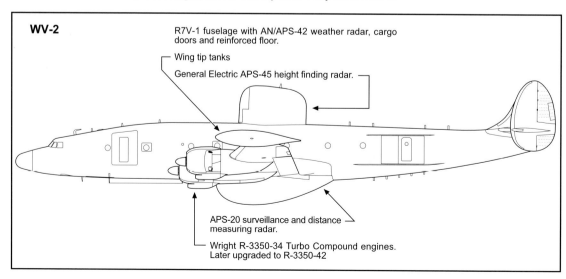

WV-2

R7V-1 fuselage with AN/APS-42 weather radar, cargo doors and reinforced floor.

Wing tip tanks

General Electric APS-45 height finding radar.

APS-20 surveillance and distance measuring radar.

Wright R-3350-34 Turbo Compound engines. Later upgraded to R-3350-42

simultaneously broadcast on two televison channels and on medium wave, short wave and FM radio. A live studio capability was incorporated along with the necessary power sources, equipment and antennae for television and radio transmission.

VC-121J: Four R7V-1/C-121Js converted to staff transports; BuAer 128443 (c/n 4110), 131623 (c/n 4124), 131624 (c/n 4125) and 131635 (c/n 4136).

EC-121K: September 1962 redesignation of WV-2.

JC-121K: One EC-121K (BuAer 143196) transferred on loan to the US Army from August 1961 to observe and track test firings of ground launched missiles. The WV-2/EC-121K radomes were removed and a cupola added to the top of the fuselage for the installation of infra-red and optical tracking equipment. Cameras were also installed. The 'J' designation prefix indicated an aircraft temporarily modified for test work that could be easily returned to its original configuration.

NEC-121K: WV-2/EC-121K BuAer 128324 modified for testing purposes, the 'N' in the designation indicating the aircraft had undergone major alterations that precluded it from being returned to original configuration. BuAer 128324 was subsequently further modified to YEC-121K and NC-121K standards (see below).

NC-121K: Special missions modifications of four EC-121Ks (BuAer 131388, 141292, 141297, 141325) plus NEC-121K BuAer 128324. All served into the 1970s.

YEC-121K: WV-2/EC-121K/NEC-121K BuAer 128324 (c/n 4304) when used to service test new equipment, thus the 'Y' (for prototype/evaluation) prefix. This much modified aircraft was subsequently further converted to NC-121K standards before being withdrawn from use in 1974.

EC-121L: September 1962 redesignation of the WV-2E (BuAer 126512) AEW test aircraft with dish radome.

EC-121M: September 1962 redesignation of the eight WV-2Qs.

WC-121N: September 1962 redesignation of WV-3.

EC-121P: Six EC-121Ks (BuAer 141296, 141306, 141328, 143189, 143199, 143200) redesignated after the installation of upgraded submarine detection equipment. The first three were transferred to the USAF in January 1967 as EC-121Rs with new serial numbers and the last three in 1966-67 as JEC-121Ps, these retaining their USN serial numbers.

JEC-121P: Three EC-121Ps transferred to the USAF in 1966-67 for avionics systems testing duties (see above).

US Air Force

The US Air Force was the second largest customer for new Constellations (after the US Navy and just ahead of TWA), taking delivery of 142 of all models from the production line including 118 Super Constellation variants. To those can be added 32 USN R7V-1 transports which were later transferred to the USAF as the C-121G, along with 39 EC-121Ks and some others which had also originally been delivered to the USN.

Like the USN, the USAF's Super Constellations were delivered to fill two primary roles: transport (C-121C/G) and airborne early warning (RC-121C/D). Many other subvariants were created by conversion to fill a number of secondary roles.

Air National Guard units began receiving ex USAF Super Constellations from 1962 as front line service began to wind down, most units keeping some aircraft until the early 1970s with some remaining on strength until the end of the decade.

C-121C: Actually the third Super Constellation variant to enter USAF service (after the RC-121C/D AEW models), the C-121C transport was

ordered in 1951 for service with the Military Air Transport Service and its long haul operations. Thirty-three were ordered, these carrying the Lockheed model number L.1049F.

The C-121C combined features of the Navy's R7V-1 and the commercial L.1049D including Turbo Compound engines, large freight doors and reinforced cabin floor. One obvious external difference to the R7V-1 was the installation of a greater number of rectangular (rather than circular) cabin windows, the same as those fitted to the commercial models.

The C-121C's engines were the more powerful R-3350-34 Turbo Compounds, these the military equivalent to the L.1649A Starliner's powerplants and each producing 3,400hp (2,535kW). Maximum takeoff weight was 135,000lb (61,236kg).

The C-121Cs were allocated the serial numbers 54-0151 to 51-0183 (c/n 4170-4202) and delivered between June 1955 and May 1956. Most had been withdrawn from service by 1972-73 although a few remained until near the end of the decade with Air National Guard or Air Force Reserve units. Many had in the meantime been converted to specialist variants.

RC-121C Warning Star: The 10 RC-121C airborne early warning (AEW) aircraft delivered to the USAF in the first half of 1953 were similar to the USN's WV-2, although they lacked that model's wingtip fuel tanks. The aircraft were built within the early WV-2 production sequence and were for all intents and purposes the same aircraft.

The RC-121C entered service with Air Defense Command in October 1953, flying patrols of the US west coast with the 552nd Wing. Most were subsequently converted to other models and the survivors were withdrawn from service in 1968-69. Serial numbers were 51-3836 to 51-3845 (c/n 4112-4121).

EC-121C: Redesignation of RC-121C from 1962, the 'E' signifying the aircraft's special electronics installation.

JC-121C: Two C-121Cs (54-1060 and 54-0178) and one RC-121C/TC-121C (51-3841) modified for electronic systems testing.

TC-121C: Nine of the ten RC-121Cs redesignated to indicate their status as crew trainers.

VC-121C: Four C-121Cs converted to VIP transports for use by the 1254th Air Transport Squadron (Special Missions) based in Washington DC.

RC-121D Warning Star: The USAF followed its initial 10 RC-121Cs with 72 RC-121Ds, these differing from their predecessors mainly in having wingtip fuel tanks. RC-121D deliveries began in August 1954 and were completed in October 1956. They served with Air Defense Command's

Thirty-two US Navy R7V-1 transports were transferred to the USAF as C-121Gs in June 1958 and issued with new serial numbers. This is 54-4063 (c/n 4139), the former USN BuAer 131638, photographed in January 1967.

551st Wing, undertaking patrols over the Atlantic Ocean. One additional RC-121D was converted from a C-121C.

EC-121D: 1962 redesignation of the RC-121D.

NC-121D: One USN WV-2 (BuAer 143226) transferred to the USAF in August 1962 as NC-121D 56-6956 for use in the TRAP III (Terminal Radiation Airborne Programme). With its above and below fuselage radomes and other operational equipment removed, the aircraft was fitted with electronic and optical sensors on top of the fuselage, these used to measure radiation emitted by bodies re-entering the earth's atmosphere at high speed. The aircraft was retired in late 1969.

VC-121E: The sole VC-121E (53-7885) started life as an R7V-1 for the US Navy (BuAer131650) but was converted on the production line as a VIP transport for presidential use. Externally, it featured airliner style rectangular cabin windows rather than the R7V-1's circular 'portholes'.

Inside, the modifications were substantial including appropriate furnishings plus extensive communications equipment for use by the president. When the president was aboard, the aircraft used the callsign 'Air Force One'.

The VC-121E was delivered to the USAF on 24 November 1954 and was used by President Eisenhower as *Columbine III*. It served as a presidential transport into the Kennedy era before being replaced by a Boeing VC-137C in October 1962. After that, the aircraft flew with the 89th Military Airlift Group until being donated to the USAF Museum at Wright-Patterson AFB, Dayton, Ohio in April 1966.

YC-121F: Two of the four US Navy R7V-2 testbeds for the Pratt & Whitney T34 turboprop (and for the evaluation of turboprop operations generally) were transferred to the USAF before delivery as 53-8157 and 53-8158 (c/n 4161-4162). Delivered in March 1955, the aircraft were evaluated operationally by being deployed on scheduled transport services with the Military Air Transport Service's Continental Division.

C-121G: Thirty-two R7V-1 transports transferred from the USN to the USAF in June 1958, redesignated and given the new serial numbers 54-4048 to 54-4079.

TC-121G: Three C-121Gs (54-4050, -4051 and -4058) modified as crew trainers.

VC-121G: One C-121G modified as a VIP transport.

EC-121H: Designation applied to 42 RC/EC-121Ds fitted with upgraded electronic and computer equipment which allowed data to be fed directly into North American Air Defense Command's Semi-Automatic Ground Environment (SAGE) system.

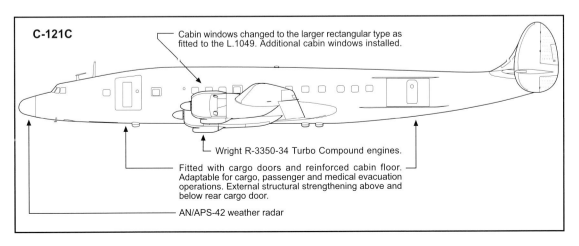

C-121C

Cabin windows changed to the larger rectangular type as fitted to the L.1049. Additional cabin windows installed.

Wright R-3350-34 Turbo Compound engines.

Fitted with cargo doors and reinforced cabin floor. Adaptable for cargo, passenger and medical evacuation operations. External structural strengthening above and below rear cargo door.

AN/APS-42 weather radar

EC-121J: Two EC-121Ds with electronics upgrades.

EC-121Q: Four EC-121D/EC-121Hs fitted with upgraded electronic intelligence gathering and countermeasures equipment.

EC-121R: Thirty USN EC-121Ks and EC-121Ps were transferred to the USAF in 1967 for use in Vietnam. Given the new serial numbers 67-21471 to 67-21500, the aircraft had their radomes and AEW equipment removed and were used as airborne relay stations for the transmission of data from the Air Delivered Seismic Intrusion Devices (ADSID) system. This sensitive movement detection equipment was dropped behind Viet Cong and North Vietnamese lines in order to identify troop and vehicle movements. Once detected, air strikes against the targets were arranged.

The EC-121R was operated by the 553rd Reconnaissance Wing flying from Thailand. The aircraft wore South-East Asia camouflage colour schemes.

EC-121S: Five C-121Cs modified in the late 1960s to EC-121Q standards with upgraded electronic intelligence gathering and countermeasures

The USAF's C-121C transport differed from the Navy's R7V-1 externally by having rectangular cabin windows rather than circular units. The delivery of 33 C-121Cs began in June 1955.

The one-off VC-121E 53-7885 *Columbine III* (c/n 4151) VIP transport was delivered in November 1954 and used by President Eisenhower.

'NASA 421', one of two R7V-1/C-121Gs operated by the National Aeronautics and Space Administration. It was 54-4076 (c/n 4159) and transferred to NASA in 1963.

One of three NC-121Js converted from R7V-1/C-121Js as airborne television and radio studio/transmitter aircraft for use in Vietnam.

equipment. They were operated by the Pennsylvania Air National Guard's Tactical Electronic Warfare Group until 1979 as the last Constellations in regular US military service.

EC-121T: Fifteen EC-121Ds and seven EC-121Hs with upgraded AEW equipment and operated by Air Force Reserve Units until 1978.

Other Military Users

India and Indonesia both acquired former airline Constellations for military use. The Indian Air Force's were all ex Air India aircraft, obtained in 1961-62 and comprising two L.1049Cs, three L.1049Es and four L.1049Gs. They were used for transport and search-and-rescue duties before five of them (two Cs, two Es and one G) were transferred to the Indian Navy in 1976 to continue performing the SAR role. They were retired in 1984 as the last military Constellations in service.

Indonesia obtained one L.1049C and two L.1049H Super Constellations in 1969, these all donated by the Pakistan Government after their retirement from Pakistan International Airlines service.

L.1649A Starliner

Lockheed had investigated turboprop versions of the L.1049 for the US military in the early 1950s through the R7V-2 (US Navy) and YC-121F (USAF) prototypes of 1954-55 (see 'Military Supers' chapter), these powered by the 5,700eshp (4,250kW) Pratt & Whitney T34 engine.

They were not proceeded with, but Lockheed kept the turboprop concept briefly alive with its L.1449 project for the commercial market with either Pratt & Whitney PT2F-1 or Rolls-Royce Tyne engines. The L.1449 also featured a lengthened fuselage, substantially increased fuel capacity and an entirely new wing of increased span, area and high aspect ratio (12 to 1) incorporating a thinner, almost laminar flow aerofoil section.

The wing's planform was completely different from that of other Constellations, replacing the slightly swept back leading edge, almost straight trailing edge and rounded outer panels/tips configuration with a straight tapered design featuring square tips and slightly forward swept trailing edges.

The turboprop Constellation never achieved production, but the new wing and some other features of the L.1449 were incorporated in the last of the line, the L.1649A Starliner.

Originally and briefly known as the 'Super Star Constellation', the Starliner was developed at the request of TWA and was a direct response to the Douglas DC-7C 'Seven Seas' which had been ordered by a dozen airlines and entered service with Pan American in June 1956.

Too late to make a substantial impact on the market at a time when the major airlines were starting to look at and order the new generation of jets, and entering service nearly a year behind the DC-7C, only 44 Starliners were built.

The DC-7C was the last of the Douglas piston engined line and featured many modifications over its predecessor DC-7B including the important one of having sufficient fuel capacity to comfortably fly the vital trans-Atlantic route non stop in both directions. Both the DC-7B and the L.1049G Super Constellation were normally incapable of flying this route non stop when travelling east-west against the prevailing wind.

The L.1649A Starliner was the final Constellation variant to be developed with a new wing, increased fuel capacity and many other modifications to compete with the Douglas DC-7C. Pictured is F-BHBK Lafayette (c/n 1011) of Air France, delivered in June 1957.

The first Starliner (N1649, c/n 1001) flew on 10 October 1956 and was retained by Lockheed. It was developed at TWA's request as a response to the Douglas DC-7C but entered service nearly a year behind its rival. For a time the Starliner was the longest range airliner in the world.

Development of the Starliner began in May 1955. Fundamentally, it combined the Super Constellation's fuselage, tail surfaces and R-3350 Turbo Compound powerplants (in slightly more powerful form) with the new wing.

The Starliner's fuel capacity was 9,278 USgal (35,120 l) or some 20 per cent greater than the L.1049G with tip tanks and range with a full load of passengers and some freight was about 1,000nm (1,850km) more. With a payload of 17,000lb (7,710kg) - sufficient for a typical load of 71 passengers and their baggage plus some additional freight - the Starliner had a range of 4,600nm (8,520km) cruising at nearly 300 knots (555km/h), this sufficient to bring every European capital city within non stop range of New York.

Maximum takeoff weight was 156,000lb (70,762kg), 18,500lb (8,392kg) greater than the L.1049G/H Super Constellation.

The Starliner was the longest range airliner in the world at the time, capable of flying more than 1,000nm (1,850km) further than even the DC-7C.

The new wing also resulted in the 3,400hp (2,535kW) R-3350-TC18-EA2 Turbo Compound engines being mounted five feet (1.5m) further outboard, this in combination with additional soundproofing and lower geared propellers helping to reduce cabin noise and vibration. The new wing was also manufactured differently, its large machined parts resulting in an almost one piece structure that required fewer parts and also had an improved strength-to-weight ratio.

Although the Starliner's fuselage was ostensibly the same as the Super Constellation's, it incorporated some alterations in order to cope with increased weights and to accommodate the new wing, which was attached to a cutout under the fuselage rather than to a conventional centre section.

The prototype L.1649 Starliner (N1649, c/n 1001) first flew on 10 October 1956, this aircraft remaining with Lockheed until 1971 when it

was sold to American Jet Industries. It was then sold to Japan where it became a restaurant and later part of an amusement park.

The production L.1649A Starliner entered service with TWA in May 1957 on the prestigious 'Blue Riband' North Atlantic route. Major rival Pan Am had introduced the DC-7C on the same route nearly a year earlier, in June 1956.

TWA followed this with an over-the-pole service between Los Angeles and London in early October 1957, the 4,780nm (8,850km) journey taking just over 18° hours to complete. Pan Am had launched a similar service three weeks earlier with the DC-7C, although TWA's Starliners were much faster on the route.

Other long range routes quickly followed including from April 1958 Air France's over-the-pole service linking Paris with Tokyo via a refuelling stop at Anchorage. Several impressive long distance delivery flights were performed including an Air France Starliner covering the 5,040nm (9,335km) between Burbank and Paris non stop in a record breaking 17hrs 11min, while Lufthansa's first aircraft flew the 6,080nm (11,260km) between Burbank and Hamburg in 17hrs 19min.

TWA operated most of the 43 Starliners which were delivered to customers, receiving 29 including four reallocated from a cancelled Alitalia order. The only other customers for new aircraft were Air France (10) and Lufthansa (4) Brazil's Varig cancelled its order for three in favour of additional Super Constellations.

The first of 29 Starliners for TWA, N7301C *Star of Wyoming* **(c/n 1002). TWA introduced the new airliner to service in May 1957 on the trans-Atlantic route but began disposing of its fleet less than three years later as the jets began arriving.**

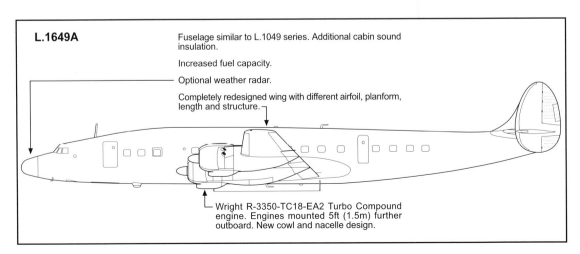

L.1649A

Fuselage similar to L.1049 series. Additional cabin sound insulation.

Increased fuel capacity.

Optional weather radar.

Completely redesigned wing with different airfoil, planform, length and structure.

Wright R-3350-TC18-EA2 Turbo Compound engine. Engines mounted 5ft (1.5m) further outboard. New cowl and nacelle design.

The last Starliner (F-BHBT, c/n 1045) was handed over to Air France in February 1958, the aircraft's modest production run belying its impressive capabilities and resulting from its relatively late start. The Starliner was outlasted in production by its predecessor, the final Super Constellation rolling off the line in late 1958.

TWA began disposing of its Starliners as early as 1959 as Boeing 707 jets came on line and had effectively retired the type by the end of 1962. Some had in the meantime been converted to freighters. Air France's fleet was withdrawn by late 1963 and Lufthansa's four aircraft were all gone by early 1964.

Second hand Starliners were subsequently flown by operators such as Aero Condor Colombia, the Flying Ambassadors Travel Club, International Travel Club, Holiday Wings, World Airways, Trans Atlantica Argentina, Air Afrique, Trek Airways, Condor Flugdienst and Luxair. Most had been retired by the late 1960s but a couple survived in service until the early 1980s.

The Lockheed Starliner can lay claim to being the 'ultimate' piston engined airliner, at least in the sense of those used by major airlines on international routes. It represented the end of an era of intense rivalry between Lockheed and Douglas which had seen both manufacturers developing ever more capable versions of their products.

Meanwhile, Boeing had been getting on with facing the challenges of the future by developing the 707 jet. The company was poised to spark another revolution in commercial air travel and was effectively leaving both Lockheed and Douglas behind as they concentrated on stretching development of the Super Constellation and DC-7 families to the limit.

Douglas finally responded to the 707 with the DC-8, but for Lockheed it would be more than a decade before its first jetliner - the L-1011 TriStar - appeared, and that would be the last airliner produced by the company.

L.1649A STARLINER

Powerplants: Four 3,400hp (2,535kW) Wright R-3350-TC18-EA2 Turbo Compound 18-cylinder radials; Hamilton-Standard or Curtiss three bladed propellers of 15ft 2in (4.62m) diameter. Fuel capacity 9,278 USgal (35,120 l).

Dimensions: Wing span 150ft 0in (45.72m); length 116ft 2in (35.41m); height 23ft 5in (7.14m); wing area 1,850sq ft (171.9m²).

Weights: Empty 85,262lb (38,675kg); max takeoff 156,000lb (70,762kg); max landing 123,000lb (55,793kg); max payload 24,355lb (11,047kg).

Accommodation: Typically 58-64 passengers in single (first) class layout, 71 in two classes or up to 91 all economy class. Underfloor freight/luggage capacity 728cu ft (20.6m³) in two holds.

Performance: Max speed 324kt (600km/h) at 18,600ft; max cruise 297kt (550km/h) at 22,600ft; normal cruise 276kt (511km/h) at 15,000ft; initial climb 1,080ft (329m)/min; service ceiling 23,700ft; max payload range 4,293nm (7,950km), range with 17,000lb (7,710kg) payload 4,600nm (8,520kg); range with 8,000lb (3,630kg) payload 5,370nm (9,945km); max range 5,983nm (11,080km).

The Starliner's completely new high aspect ratio wing is well shown in this shot of the prototype parked next to a Qantas Super Constellation.

Appendices

Summary of Deliveries

Notes: The table summarises Constellation, Super Constellation and Starliner deliveries to initial customers (including military), noting the operator, model, quantity and date of first delivery. It does not cover cancellations or resales.

Customer	Model	Qty	1st Deliv	Notes
Aerlinte Eireann	749	5	Aug 1947	converted to 749A
Air Finance Corporation	1049H	3	May 1957	leased to Flying Tiger (2), Transocean (1)
Air France	049	4	June 1946	
	749	9	April 1947	7 converted to 749A
	749A	10	Jan 1950	
	1049C	10	June 1953	9 converted to 1049E
	1049G	14	July 1955	
	1649A	10	June 1957	
Air India	749	3	Feb 1948	converted to 749A
	749A	4	Oct 1949	
	1049C	2	April 1954	
	1049E	3	Jan 1955	converted to 1049G
	1049G	5	Dec 1956	
American Overseas	049	7	March 1946	
Avianca	749A	2	May 1951	
	1049E	3	Aug 1954	
	1049G	1	Nov 1955	
BOAC	C-69/049	5	April 1946	
California Eastern Aviation	1049H	5	April 1957	leased to TWA (3), Transcontinental (2)
Chicago & Southern	649A	6	Aug 1950	converted to 749A
Cubana	1049E	1	Nov 1954	
	1049G	3	Feb 1956	
Dollar Associates	1049H	1	May 1957	leased to Transocean
Eastern Air Lines	649	14	March 1947	13 converted to 749A
	749A	7	Sept 1949	
	1049	14	Nov 1951	
	1049C	16	Nov 1953	
	1049G	10	Sept 1956	
Flying Tiger Line	1049H	13	Feb 1957	
Hughes Tool Co	749A	1	June 1951	sold to BOAC 1954
	1049G	1	Feb 1956	stored, resold 1960
	1049G	1	May 1956	leased to TWA
Iberia	1049E	3	June 1954	converted to 1049G
	1049G	2	July 1957	
KLM Royal Dutch Airlines	049	6	May 1946	
	749	11	Aug 1947	7 converted to 749A
	749A	9	Oct 1948	
	1049C	9	June 1953	
	1049E	4	May 1954	converted to 1049G
	1049G	6	Dec 1955	
	1049H	3	April 1958	
L A Venezolana	049	2	Oct 1946	
	749	2	Sept 1947	
	1049E	2	Oct 1954	1 converted to 1049G
	1049G	2	Feb 1956	
	1049H	3	April 1958	

Customer	Model	Qty	1st Deliv	Notes
Lufthansa	1049G	8	March 1955	
	1649A	4	Sept 1957	
National Airlines	1049H	4	Sept 1957	
Northwest Orient	1049G	4	April 1955	
Pakistan International	1049C	3	Feb 1954	
	1049H	2	Feb 1958	
Pan American Airways	049	20	Jan 1946	converted to 749A
	749	5	June 1947	1 leased from Lockheed
Pan American Grace	049	2	May 1946	
Qantas	749	4	Oct 1947	converted to 749A
	1049C	4	March 1954	converted to 1049E
	1049E	6	Jan 1955	5 converted to 1049G
	1049G	4	Oct 1955	
	1049H	2	Oct 1956	
REAL SA	1049H	4	Feb 1958	
Resort Airlines	1049H	2	May 1957	leased to TWA
Seaboard & Western	1049D	4	Aug 1954	3 converted to 1049H
	1049H	5	Dec 1956	
Slick Airways	1049H	1	Sept 1957	
South African Airways	749A	4	April 1950	
TAP Portugal	1049G	3	July 1955	
Thai Airways	1049G	3	July 1957	
Trans-Canada Airlines	1049C	5	Feb 1954	converted to 1049E
	1049E	3	June 1954	
	1049G	4	April 1956	
	1049H	2	Dec 1958	
TWA	C-69/049	27	Nov 1945	
	749	12	March 1948	
	749A	25	March 1950	
	1049	10	May 1952	
	1049G	27	March 1955	
	1049H	6	March 1958	
	1649A	29	May 1957	
US Air Force	C-69	14	April 1944	
	C-121A	9	Nov 1948	
	VC-121B	1	Nov 1948	
	C-121C	33	June 1955	
	RC-121C	10	Jan 1953	for conversions see text
	RC-121D	72	Aug 1954	for conversions see text
	VC-121E	1	Nov 1954	'Columbine III'
	YC-121F	2	March 1955	turboprop testbed
US Navy	PO-1W	2	Aug 1949	redesignated WV-1
	R7V-1	50	Nov 1952	32 to USAF as C-121G
	R7V-2	2	Dec 1953	turboprop testbeds
	WV-2	142	March 1954	for conversions see text
	WV-3	8	April 1956	for conversions see text
Varig	1049G	6	May 1955	

Constructor's Numbers

Lockheed used distinctive series of constructor's numbers for most of the main Constellation, Super Constellation and Starliner models, as summarised below. Note that the number ranges include airframes for which numbers were allocated but were not built or reallocated. They therefore do not necessarily accurately reflect production quantities.

c/n 1001-1047.................... L.1649A
c/n 1961-2088.................... L.049/C-69

```
c/n 2501-2673.................... L.649/A, L.749/A, C-121A/B, PO-1W
c/n 4001-4024.................... L.1049
c/n 4101-4499.................... R7V-1/2, WV-2/3, C/RC-121C/D/F/G, L.1049D
c/n 4501-4687.................... L.1049C/E/G
c/n 4801-4853.................... L.1049H
c/n 5500-5522.................... WV-2 final batch
```

US Air Force Serial Numbers

C-69: 42-94549/9460 (42-94554/94560 not taken up; 43-10309 (prototype); 43-10310/10317.
C/VC-121A: 48-0609/48-0617.
VC-121B: 48-0608.
C-121C: 54-0151/54-0183.
RC-121C: 51-3836/51-3845.
RC-121D: 52-3411/52-3425; 53-0553/53-0556; 53-3398/53-3403; 54-2304/54-2308; 55-0118/55-0139.
VC-121E: 53-7885.
YC-121F: 53-8157/53-8158.
C-121G: 54-4048/54-4079 (ex USN R7V-1).
EC-121R: 67-21471/67-21500 (ex USN WV-3/EC-121P and WV-2/EC-121K).

US Navy Serial Numbers

PO-1W/WV-1: 124437-124438.
R7V-1: 128434-128444; 131621-131629; 131632-131649; 131651-59; 140311-140313.
R7V-2: 131630-131631.
WV-2: 126512-126513; 128323-128326; 131387-131392; 135746-135761; 137887-137890; 141289-141333;   143184-143230;   145924-145941.
WV-3: 137891-137898.

Production Summary

L.049/C-69	88
L.649	14
L.649A	6
L.749	51
L.749A	62
C-121A/B	10
PO-1W/WV-1	2
L1049	24
L.1049C	49
L.1049D	4
L.1049E	25
L.1049G	104
L.1049H	53
R7V-1/C-121G	50
R7V-2	2
WV-2	142
WV-3	8
C-121C	33
RC-121C	10
RC-121D	72
VC-121E	1
YC-121F	2
L.1649A	44
Total	**856**

LIMITED EDITION AVIATION ART POSTERS

Limited edition, **quality colour collectable posters** with artwork by internationally renowned aviation artist **Juanita Franzi**. The colour posters are printed on quality 200 gsm art board and are ideal for framing or mounting. They are of a manageable size (B3, 500 mm x 353 mm) with each of the five images approximately 25-26 cm long. Five quality drawings for the price of one.

An ideal adornment for the study, office or club house. The perfect gift for the aviation enthusiast.

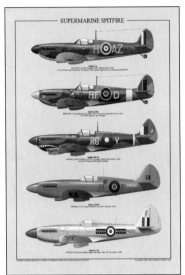
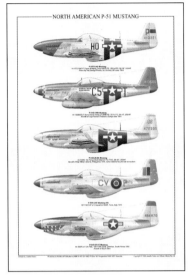

Supermarine Spitfire: The five drawings represent the evolution and development of arguably the world's most famous and charismatic fighter. The five drawings depict the Mks. I, V, VIII, XIX and 22 ranging from a Battle of Britain aircraft to Wng Cdr Bobby Gibbes' RAAF Mk.VIII and a post war Mk.22.

North American P-51 Mustang: The USA's most famous fighter of WWII is celebrated by drawings of the P-51Ds of 8th Air Force aces Maj George Preddy and Capt Richard Peterson plus 5th Air Force ace Maj William Shomo, Korean War pilot Maj P Dow and a Royal Australian Air Force P-51K.

McDonnell Douglas F-4 Phantom: One of the most significant and effective combat aircraft of any era, Mr Mac's 'Phabulous Phantom' is represented by drawings of a USN F-4B, a Vietnam era USAF F-4D, the famous 'Playboy Bunny' F-4J, a Royal Navy FG.1 and a Royal Australian Air Force F-4E.

LIMITED EDITION AVIATION POSTERS ONLY $A20.00 each (GST included)
Postage and handling $A4.00 per order in Australia (overseas $A8.00)
Please allow two weeks for delivery in Australia.

VISIT OUR WEB SITE AND GET THE LATEST INFORMATION ON PRODUCTS AND EVENTS
WWW.NOTEBOOKPUB.COM

Or mail us at:

Notebook Publications (ABN 94 082 531 066)
PO Box 181, Bungendore NSW 2621 Australia
Telephone: +61 2 6238 1620   Facsimile: +61 2 6238 1626

Stewart Wilson's newest book series:

Aviation Notebook Series: 1.   McDonnell Douglas F-4 Phantom by Stewart Wilson
2.   Boeing 747 by Stewart Wilson
3.   BAe/MDC Harrier by Stewart Wilson
4.   Lockheed Constellation by Stewart Wilson